PN3448 .[

W9-DBQ-184

Winks, Robin W.

Modus operandi

MODUS OPERANDI

MODUS OPERANDI

AN EXCURSION INTO DETECTIVE FICTION

Robin W. Winks

DAVID R. GODINE, PUBLISHER
BOSTON

The Publisher is grateful for permission to reprint:

excerpts from "Thirteen Ways of Looking at a Blackbird"
and "The Idea of Order at Key West" from THE COLLECTED
POEMS OF WALLACE STEVENS. Copyright © 1954 by Wallace
Stevens. Reprinted by permission of Alfred A. Knopf, Inc.

"The Arrival of the Bee Box" from ARIEL by Sylvia Plath.
Copyright © 1963, 1965 by Ted Hughes. Reprinted by permission
of Harper & Row, Publishers, Inc. and Faber & Faber, London.

"Richard Cory" by Edwin Arlington Robinson from Edwin
Arlington Robinson, *The Children of the Night.* Copyright
under the Berne Convention. Reprinted with the permission
of Charles Scribner's Sons.

First published in 1982 by
David R. Godine, Publisher, Inc.
306 Dartmouth Street, Boston, Massachusetts 02116

Copyright © 1982 by Robin W. Winks

Library of Congress Cataloging in Publication Data
Winks, Robin W.
Modus operandi.
1. Detective and mystery stories—History and criticism. I. Title.
PN3448.D4W5   809.3'872   81-81446
ISBN 0-87923-406-7   AACR2
Printed in the United States of America

To
WINNIE-THE-POOH,
who made all things possible, and to
ALEXANDER SMITH,
utterly forgotten, whose motto is inscribed
on my ashtray (though I don't smoke):
"Everything is sweetened by risk"

ACKNOWLEDGMENTS

The idea for so personal an essay as this came from the fertile wisdom of William B. Goodman, while the title is owed to his assistant, Nikki Sklare, who had the good sense to graduate from Yale in 1976. My daughter, Honor, helped type the manuscript and complained of its prose, with good reason, and my wife, Avril, undertook to renew her pledge never to read a word I write about detective fiction. My son, Eliot, says he will read the book one day, though he is rather busy just now, and my father will accept a free copy. All have helped me write this book by remarking that they did not much like my last work of "serious scholarship," which was on the British Empire. Our dog, Bark, which someone else is supposed to walk, delayed the book measurably by making demands upon me twice a day. I also wish to thank Laphroig, a late-night companion from Scotland.

MODUS OPERANDI

1

A N *excursion:* an escape from bounds; an outburst; a journey, usually for pleasure or health, made with the intention of returning; a deviation. Just so might one best explore detective fiction; indeed, not "best" but "must," since it is most likely to be dismissed by those who profess to take their fiction seriously. To be serious, if not solemn, about detective fiction is beyond the bounds of most modern literary criticism. To be heard, that small band (not so small) who tell all the truth but tell it slant must shout out, sallying forth with hyperbole, claiming for Agatha Christie qualities others would hardly dare claim for John Milton, destroying their case by excess. Here the mystery buff tries to enlist T. S. Eliot through *Murder in the Cathedral*; there the ponderous defender of his private pleasure tells us that John D. MacDonald is a doorway into Jung's collective unconscious; over there, faintly to be seen in the middle distance, the critic of society finds the other Macdonald, Ross, is illustrating Freud's *Totem and Taboo*, as the memory of the father is killed by a band of brothers; and right here before our very eyes a respected reviewer suggests, and by suggesting loses the respect of his tribe, that G. K. Chesterton's Father Brown stories and Charles Dickens's *Great Expectations* have so much in common they must be styled "mystery romances." Such views, pleasurable as they are, and as good for our literary health as they may be, must strike many readers as deviations from the received wisdom. After all, as we are told, there are at least *some* standards that may even yet be upheld: "King Lear is in, Tarzan is out," so far as quality is concerned. In the end, those who try to analyze detective fiction according to the language of academic criticism sound shrill, foolish, or simply sad, forgetting as they have that the truth must dazzle gradually, or every man be blind.

Now right there is one of the problems: High Brow is expected to recognize having had Emily Dickinson thrown at him twice in one paragraph; Middle Brow will suspect that something is going on of a rather baroque nature in the paragraph now behind us; and we are supposed to assume that Low Brow will not have the slightest notion that the paragraph has been out behind the barn at games. One approach to justifying the serious reading of detective fiction is to show that one may keep company with the allusive critic at his best, while another approach is to suggest straight out that one is not slumming simply because semen stains on the sheets tell us something. Because we generally couple *mystery*, at least in American fiction, with the modifier *murder*, we consign the genre to Low Brow activities as enjoyed by Middle Brow voyeurs, and John Milton gets crowded out. Precisely because mystery and detective fiction deal with society's deepest fears, we prefer to keep the very artifacts in which those fears are embedded —and, yes, exploited—buried amid the underliterature of our culture. In the end, we are missing out on an entire set of clues—those shelves upon shelves of books hidden at the back of the stacks in Cape Cod community libraries, under the terse heading "mysteries"—which most reveal the modus operandi of modern America.

Of course, even though we generally speak of murder mysteries, and especially so in the United States, often such books do not deal with what the law defines as murder. Manslaughter, accident followed by cover-up, and other crimes confused by the puzzles we associate with the genre are generally swept into the same classification. The English feel less compulsion to murder, in art as in life: there are no murders in many of Dick Francis's dependably realistic mysteries set in the world of horse racing, and no one is killed in Dorothy Sayers's masterwork, *Gaudy Night*. Nor does Amanda Cross, American, feel it un- civilized to murder no one as she pursues her poetic justice. The New York bookstore Murder Ink sells many books that contain no murders. Some aficionados feel com- pelled to draw sharp distinctions between murder mysteries, detective fiction, espionage thrillers, and so on, and given that people die in some books and not in others, the distinctions may be said to be real. In art, however, the question of murder as defined by the law does not seem an element essential, even though common, to the body of literature embraced by the subtitle of this essay. I prefer to let a hundred flowers bloom, and I do not intend to worry here (since there are several German doctoral dissertations that do the worrying for me) about drawing fine lines between categories within the literature. I shall refer to subsets of the genre from time to time while treating it as I see it: as a continuum, a logical passage, a whole.

One wants to avoid the vice of believing in "placing," even as any critic will certainly place a writer amid his vision of life. This is an intensely personal essay; it does not seek to "cover" the field, "fill a gap," "survey a scene," or provide a theory of literary criticism. It is precisely as advertised: an excursion.

2

THERE ARE PEOPLE who like baseball and people who like football. There are those who read science fiction and those who go on stakeout with Ed Mc-Bain. There are those who are interested in what they see, in what is there, and there are those who are most interested in what they cannot see, in what ought to be but isn't there. There are those (sometimes called "liberals") who think about the world as they would like it to be, and there are those (sometimes called "conservatives") who care most about the hard, plain facts of the world as it is. There are those who assume people are roughly what they appear to be and those who are certain that every utterance contains a subtext and every facial twitch a confession. There are those who would absolve us from our mediocrity and those who know that mediocrity is too fascinating to wish away. And there are those who run from the Hound of Heaven while there are others who attract guilt like a magnet.

The world is no simple dichotomy, and most of us would mix and match a bit in this cluster of oppositions. We are, after all, either lumpers or splitters, and in the lumpen-proletariat of the mind, all of the above categories fall to the former. But lumping and splitting are not wrong ways to look at life per se, and if they help a person come to terms with an environment, if they make it possible to knock that environment about a bit with the elbows and make it take a shape a bit more comfortable for one's needs, so that one can go out and pursue other wants so deep that they become needs, who is to say that lumping and splitting are not effective, and certainly accessible and cheap, ways of achieving what the psychiatrists tell us we all need: a path into personal psychoanalysis.

Mystery fiction apparently fills some deep need for some of us, or it would not be so widely read. One in four books purchased in the United States today, leaving out the compelled purchase at the college textbook counter, is a murder mystery, detective story, spy thriller, or gothic romance—not the same things, though extensions of the same concerns. Walk through any crowded airplane en route between airports stamped from identical molds and you will find those passengers who are not sleeping, at gin rummy, or hassling a stewardess, deep into a book, and for two-thirds of those literate souls, the book will be by Robert Ludlum, John le Carré, or perhaps this year P. D. James. Escapist literature? Clearly not, for most readers are being drawn deeper into the very subjects they fear most. Mindless matter? Hardly, when convolutions of plot and symbolism of action require the reader to be ever alert, ears erect and nose twitching, for the author's hidden agendas. Sublimating the fear of death? That's not what Erica Jong was writing about, and titles can mislead, as can motivations; otherwise why does one find Arthur Hailey's *Airport* a best-seller in every newsstand from Kennedy through O'Hare to Seatak? The mystery reader knows that appearances are never what they seem, and that no ritual, rôle, or action should escape interrogation.

Surely lumping is, in a rough way, correct; we do fall into personality types, and detective fiction reinforces the needs and expectations of certain types as it repels others. Look at those pairs in opposition again. Baseball, it has been said by no less an authority than a university president, is like poetry: one knows exactly what each player must attempt to do in a given situation, a set piece, of almost Oriental subtlety. Pitcher, batter, catcher, first baseman, fielders have their assigned rôles, and the spectator can anticipate what each, in sequence, will attempt. The suspense lies not in asking What Happens Next; it lies in the anticipation, in the waiting, in holding the breath to see whether that which must be done can be done. To our reader type two, the game is too static, the variables insufficient, the action potentially predictable. The entire scene is as cool and clean as a Zen poem. Beauty is in the performance, which, because predictable, may be shared. Baseball, like cricket, is for the gregarious.

Football, much the superior sport, is for the loner, all talk of teamwork only surface sheen. In football, which is a kind of brawny chess game, the variables at any given moment are enormous. To the spectator, suspense arises as much from not knowing what must happen next, or in disagreeing with coach or quarterback over what will have happened as a result of a series of events, as over the event, the play, itself. The huddle allows one's doubts, like private detectives, to search out the weaknesses in the game plan, to make out a case against action or inaction, against this choice or that. The beauty in the sport arises not from seeing that which we know must happen occur perfectly, the ball and bat in perfect harmony, the poet finding just the line to conclude the thought. Rather, it arises from the persistence of doubt, and its mounting, repetitious nature: what will happen is followed by the postmortem—should it have happened?—and by the insistent question: by this happening what new chain of cause and effect has been set in motion? Baseball appeals to our certainties, football to our uncertainties.

Living with ambiguity is not easy. Most people like their History clear and plain: they want to know the ten causes for the fall of the Roman Empire, the reasons why the middle class is always rising, and why Jack Ruby was shot, and they are convinced that there are answers that are being kept from them. Historians know that taking refuge in a list of causes is an easy substitute for thinking; they also know—even as they stalk that list, imply it, hint at it, and finally, with their arm twisted behind their back by a text-book publisher with fast bucks in hand, reduce complex events to just such a list so that undergraduates may memorize the list and thus understand History—that events are too complex, too hidden to be reduced to language. The good historian always has a subtext in hand, perhaps revealed only in the sequence in which the list of putative causes is unfolded; for while living with ambiguity is not easy, living without ambiguity is an untruth and therefore impossible. The writer of detective fiction, even more the reader of such fiction, knows that ambivalence and aliena-tion are his lot, and that he must enjoy the crying of that lot. Surely that is what Thomas Pynchon, mystery writer, was telling us.

But let us not be too pretentious, or portentous. The essence of true mystery was best captured by Henry James, who needs our attention for a moment if we are to under-stand the genre's inherent structure. In *The Turn of the Screw* James wrote one of those few short novels that virtually every high school graduate in America has been asked to read at some time. The attraction, aside from brevity, is that the book can be taught—it leaves the teacher with something, indeed many somethings, to say. One's reaction to *The Turn of the Screw* is one of the two best litmus tests I know for finding out whether one is going to lift one's eyes in maturity to detective fiction or follow the valleys of science fiction. The two tests are worth examin-ing for a moment.

The first test arises from Agatha Christie's most famous work, *The Murder of Roger Ackroyd*, first published in

1926. If the solution to the mystery makes one angry, if one feels that Miss Christie cheated, then one ought not to read another such book. If one agrees with Dorothy Sayers's spirited defense, when rule-bound critics attacked the Ackroyd resolution, "Fooled you! And Fair!" then one is ready to move on. Quite simply, Agatha Christie required of the reader two small courtesies: that one read her word for word, and that one take her at her word. At one level the second expectation is contrary to the detective reader's sense of caution as it is contrary to the historian's sense of prudence, but at a second level the expectation is precisely right: an expectation that the craftsman intended to do that which the craftsman did, and that courtesy (always the highest form of efficiency) be accorded the craftsman. The doctrine of fair play applies in both directions, after all.

But first, the context. Agatha Christie had already written five books; she had a track record, and readers were entitled to think they knew how her mind worked; she had also already attracted notoriety by her now famous and much studied (and vulgarized) disappearance. Monsignor Ronald Knox, an English essayist, Christian apologist, and author of many detective stories that helped to establish the conventional wisdom concerning the tradition of fair play in mystery fiction, had already made known through a band of friends most of his "detective story decalogue." The decalogue would be formally presented at a meeting of the Detection Club, founded in London in 1928 by the mystery author Anthony Berkeley, and published by Knox the following year. He intended his decalogue to chide certain writers, Miss Christie among them. She, in turn, would take up the challenge; and before she died, rich in age, books, and cash, she systematically broke every one of Knox's commandments, though she waited for a posthumous publication to smash the seventh one.

Knox's first commandment was that "the criminal must be someone mentioned in the early part of the story, but must not be anyone whose thoughts the reader has been allowed to follow." To be sure, Knox was writing long in advance of Robbe-Grillet, Barthes, and the structuralists, and he would not have changed his mind even had Freud himself been a member of the Detection Club, but the injunction was indefensible on the face of it, though it took Miss Christie to show its face. For—yes, if one is to discuss mystery fiction seriously, one must "give away" the plot, with no apologies to anyone so deprived as not already to have read *Roger Ackroyd*—the book opens with sympathetic, intelligent Dr. Sheppard telling the story. Not far into the book Ackroyd is found, behind the locked door to his study, slumped in an armchair before his fire, a dagger driven into his neck. We find the body, see the investigation, through the eyes of Ackroyd's personal physician, who is presented as an alert, concerned, and humane person.

One paragraph, and one alone, provides the litmus paper:

I did what little had to be done. I was careful not to disturb the position of the body, and not to handle the dagger at all. No object was to be attained by moving it. Ackroyd had clearly been dead some little time.

One sentence, earlier, prepares the acid for the paper. A letter is brought to Ackroyd at twenty minutes to nine, while Dr. Sheppard is with him; Ackroyd would clearly learn something the doctor feels he should know, at that juncture, but Ackroyd refuses to read the letter in Sheppard's presence. The sentence in question reads: "It was just on ten minutes to nine when I left him, the letter still unread."

With these lines singled out in this way, the reader may readily deduce that Dr. Sheppard is the murderer. If they were embedded skillfully in a clear though complex text, one might be inclined to attach different meanings to the sentences—indeed, the overwhelming majority of readers did then and still do, upon first encounter with the book, fail to mark the significance of these passages. Once these sentences have been remarked, a very few other phrases and sentences take on a heightened intensity of meaning, though if the reader had not chosen precisely these lines for interrogation, the others would reasonably escape notice.

Yet surely a truly alert reader would wonder, at least idly, what transpired in the ten minutes over which the sentence so easily slips, and if thus alerted, would ask what the "little [that] had to be done" might have been. The ear and eye sensitive to sentence structure ought to query the function of those words, "No object"; one might even wonder how a doctor who has not examined a body could assert that Ackroyd had "clearly" been dead for some time. Not to press an obvious point too insistently, these are precisely the questions the historian would ask of a document, the worries a logician might entertain, or the constructions in style that a literary critic might (if paying Miss Christie the courtesy of treating her as a serious professional who chose the words she intended to use with care) query. That is, as with history, law, and life, one must read the text with attention and respect.

Edmund Wilson, at the height of his powers as America's most respected literary critic, wrote a scathing essay that asked "Who Cares Who Killed Roger Ackroyd?" to a negative conclusion. Such books were boring, "rubbish," on which paper ought not, in the wartime year 1944, be "squandered." Wilson admitted that he found Christie, Dorothy Sayers, Margery Allingham, and Ngaio Marsh so bad he could not finish them; Sayers's *Nine Tailors*, "one of the dullest books" he had ever encountered, he skimmed. He would not, of course, skim Proust. Yet what is one to do with a critic who dismisses a work of fiction without reading it, and particularly a work drawn from a genre that compels attention to each word? As with history, the discrete fact counts; initially all facts must be presumed to count equally; in time a pattern emerges by which one may place priorities of significance upon facts as they relate to cause and effect. In time one discovers the modus operandi. One cannot discover it, in history, in detective fiction, or in life, by deliberately preselecting, skimming, omitting as irrelevant an experience. Perhaps detective fiction is for those of us who have never learned to read without moving our lips, for the lip will tell the brain what the eye alone cannot.

Now we may return, emboldened by context, to that figure of high culture, Henry James. Broadly speaking there are three possible ways to read *The Turn of the Screw*. Ten paperbound editions are available to the reader today; three announce, with slight variations, that the story is "perhaps the most fascinating ghost story ever written." Certainly one thriving subset of works within the broad genre of thriller fiction arises almost directly from James's story: the many books, especially popular in the 1980s, about apparently innocent children who possess the power of unspeakable evil, sexual perversity beyond imagination, who are the corrupters of mankind. Stephen King, among others, has exploited this vein, as have any number of motion pictures developed from such books: *Rosemary's Baby*, *Carrie*, the Damien series.

No such reading occurred to me when, as an early teenager, I was set this story by an unusual teacher. I was unaware that literary debate might swirl about so compelling, and to me so clear, an account of how a mad governess, progressively revealed in her madness, destroyed the essentially innocent. This second interpretation, now far more in favor though perhaps still a minority view, holds that *The Turn of the Screw* is not a ghost story at all; it is the account of the evils done by those who see the world with "certitude." An insane woman tells her story. James had done, in 1898, what Christie would do in 1926, though far more subtly, in an insidiously sustained, sly way. Or so I thought and still think.

My recollection of my reaction to a first reading of *The Turn of the Screw* brings us toward the questions I wish to put. Was I already, at thirteen, predisposed to seek "rational" explanations for events, so that I rejected without thought the possibility that I had just read one of the most fascinating ghost stories ever written? Was I, simply, a slow reader, whose eye lit upon certain words, passages, which reread by me as an adult, now alert to the controversy over interpretation, seem to stand out from the text even more clearly? (Did not the governess ask, "If he *were* innocent, what then on earth was *I?*" Were we not to take the author's questions seriously?) Did I recognize, at some level of self-consciousness, that I was dealing with a ghost story, and from some fear of the supernatural, or of death, reject this view before I even examined it, and reject it yet? Was I later, as a college student, too easily confirmed in my view by James's remarkable statement in *Portrait of a Lady* —which I read in the same year, and with the same hypnotized obsessive closeness, as Mann's *Magic Mountain* and Melville's *Moby Dick*, so that I still account that the year I came intellectually alive—that the consciousness of the artist was "the posted presence of the watcher-without"? Had I already become observer, distant, with icicle eye, or was it by the reading of just such works as these that I distanced myself? Does one become a historian because of a sense of uninvolvement, or does the sense arise from a lifetime spent being a historian?

The answer, of course, lies in the third interpretation that might be placed on James's work: that he intends to show us both possibilities and how they interact. The children do see ghosts, and the governess, who is mad, uses their evil to her own purposes, or is herself driven mad by what she perceives. Both this and the preceding view provide James with a creditable claim to have begun another popular subset within the genre of the thriller: those interminable stories of young women sent to Gothic mansions high on isolated moors, there to look after mysterious children and to be terrorized, last seen running from the turreted house into the fogs of romance. This answer, surely, fulfills the commonsense approach to history: that there is a bit of truth in most interpretations. But the commonsense approach is insufficient, for there is not an equal measure of truth in all interpretations of a discrete event, and the historian's task is to decide upon the proximate cause, the remote causes, and the relationship between two such types of separable causes. It is in the examination of the relationship that the interpretation occurs.

Not being a James scholar, I lack entitlement to comment on him *in extenso*, as the weightier books say. Still, two other thoughts seem relevant, though tangentially so, at this point. I have never seen Benjamin Britten's version of *The Turn of the Screw*, missed opportunities being the curse of the deadline-ridden, but I have listened to his opera on recordings and have read the libretto. It seems clear to me that he intends to follow the third line, showing children who, in touch with evil, are plunged further into disaster by a slyly sinful and not mad governess. The music more than the words supports this view. I still think Britten is wrong. The other thought is equally unremarkable: both detectives and historians have to establish what some phi-losophers (and many businessmen) call "an autonomous ethic," by which they decide whether a specific act in a chain of acts is ethical or not. Does the historian lie in order to gain access to a collection of papers essential to the telling of his story? Does the detective mislead the witness, falsify his identity, and fight fire with fire? In *The Aspern Papers* James says yes to both questions and then tells us why being a yea-sayer to the world is a sin. "I have failed, most miserably failed, and there is no more innocence in me"—thus Britten's governess. One ought not to fail in written history or in detective fiction; if failure is certain, one redefines the problem or asks the right question.

The historian, and James, recognizes the dangers in the presumed continuum that often reads: cause equals respon-sibility equals guilt. James writes of those interstices be-tween the watcher-without and the watched, and of how the watched, knowing he is watched, may redefine the relation-ship between the two. One is ready to give our excursion its proper place among literary travels if one is comfortable in James's House of Fiction:

> The house of fiction has . . . not one window, but a million . . . every one of which has been pierced, or is still pierceable, in its vast front, by the need of the individual vision and by the pressure of the individual will. These apertures, of dissimilar shape and size . . . are but windows at the best, mere holes in a dead wall, disconnected, perched aloft; they are not hinged doors opening straight upon life. But they have this mark of their own that at each of them stands a figure with a pair of eyes, or at least with field-glass, which forms, again and again, for observation, a unique instrument, insuring to the person making use of it an impression

distinct from every other. He and his neighbours are watching the same show, but one seeing more where the other sees less, one seeing black where the other sees white, one seeing big where the other sees small, one seeing coarse where the other sees fine. And so on, and so on. . . .

And so it goes. Vonnegut sees Dresden with the eyes of a survivor, a Churchill biographer sees its bombing as necessary to the destruction of German morale, John Hersey sees that destruction as a British Hiroshima, David Irving sees the following firestorm as a deliberate massacre, Nicolas Freeling sees it in an ironic title as Dresden Green. Where James used the field glass, today we might use the camera, as in Antonioni's *Blow-Up*, or in Dick Francis's *Reflex*, in which the camera is a shield that, his hero says, "keeps you a step away from the world. Makes you an observer. Gives you an excuse not to feel."

Our excursion along what is presumed to be the high road of the House of Fiction may soon descend to those depths Edmund Wilson dismissed so easily. (Perhaps skimming a bit too rapidly, he managed to miss one of those seemingly awkward constructions in *The Turn of the Screw* that, in its self-consciously precious choice of words, ought to have been as clear a signal to him as Agatha Christie had provided, and so his own interpretation went awry.) But let us make the point about ambiguity and appearances yet one more time, now from poetry, so that we might make peace between our first two opposites. In a statement less obscure than it seems, the poet Wallace Stevens wrote, "The accuracy of accurate letters is an accuracy with respect to the structure of reality." In his poem "The Idea of Order at Key West," he lets us see through one of James's apertures, looking back upon the key from the seaward side to find a sense of physical order that reflects an internal, emotional reordering:

> . . . when the singing ended and we turned
> Toward the town, tell why the glassy lights,
> The lights in the fishing boats at anchor there,
> As the night descended, tilting in the air,
> Mastered the night and portioned out the sea,
> Fixing emblazoned cones and fiery poles,
> Arranging, deepening, enchanting night.

There are, Stevens tells us, thirteen ways of looking at a blackbird; each shows us a path along which our excursion might move, though one more than most:

> I do not know which to prefer,
> The beauty of inflections
> Or the beauty of innuendoes,
> The blackbird whistling
> Or just after.

Distance, then, and inflection: innuendo, if you wish. With such matters mystery fiction must be comfortable. Here is John D. MacDonald describing Florida, to which (as good writers must with respect to most environments) he clearly has something of an adversary relationship:

> In the early afternoon I turned off Route 41 onto 846 and drove the small empty roads over past Corkscrew, Immokalee, Devil's Garden. The tourists were booming down the big roads, white-knuckled in the traffic, waiting for the warning signals from their Fuzzbusters, staring out at endless strips of junk stores, cypress knees, plaster herons, and instant

greasy chicken. We rumbled gently along through the wild country, watching the birds, the dangle of Spanish moss, the old ranch houses set way back under the shade trees, the broad placid faces of the Brahma cattle.

This is not stylish writing, but it does its job: it shows us the two Floridas, the one surviving even yet behind the facade of all that is finger-lickin' good, and it sets Travis McGee, our romantic hero, apart from the snowbirds, a man just a bit more aware, able to see a little more deeply the good old virtues that remain. We know that McGee will be a survivor, like those old ranch houses. Some might dismiss this as sentimental writing (and it is), as a bit vicious on the tourists who make it possible for the dangle of Spanish moss to survive (and it is), but it also provides that ambivalence, that sense of juxtaposition, that hint of being off balance, that is at the core of all thriller fiction. McGee is another detective, though amateur; another historian, though amateur; the reader who likes him will need to have an icicle in the eye too. As McGee is told by his best friend, "You are never entirely *here*. Do you know that? You are always a little way down the road. You are always fretting about consequences instead of giving yourself up totally to the present moment." Yes, he knows that, and we see ourselves in him. Detective fiction—all of it—tells us at least one simple message, though a message complex enough that most very young children and some adults do not grasp it: actions have consequences. So do myths and legends, lies and evasions; they too are forms of action. Inaction, the dog that didn't bark in the night, is no less significant.

Edwin Arlington Robinson is not much read these days; he appears to be passing out of the anthologies. One falls into the trap of allowing those who do not read detective fiction to dismiss it as trite if one leans too heavily on one of Robinson's less well-regarded poems to underscore the point about appearances, and yet, on so personal an excursion as this, perhaps it is permissible to use "Richard Cory," that poem by which I know I became a historian, a watcher, and one certain that few people are what they seem. I still have an anthology of poems I read when about ten; against this one stands a cross and my notation, ignorant of critical theory, "outstanding":

Whenever Richard Cory went down town,
    We people on the pavement looked at him:
He was a gentleman from sole to crown,
    Clean favored, and imperially slim.

And he was always quietly arrayed,
    And he was always human when he talked;
But still he fluttered pulses when he said,
    "Good-morning," and he glittered when he walked.

And he was rich—yes, richer than a king,
    And admirably schooled in every grace:
In fine, we thought that he was everything
    To make us wish that we were in his place.

So on we worked, and waited for the light,
    And went without the meat, and cursed the bread;
And Richard Cory, one calm summer night,
    Went home and put a bullet through his head.

Only years later, reasonably enough, did I discover Sylvia Plath's "Arrival of the Bee Box." It deals with that question of literary theory and philosophy, What will have happened? Let it end this excursus on the high road, for it tells

us precisely what we must expect, nuance by nuance, when
we feel zero at the bone:

I ordered this, this clean wood box
Square as a chair and almost too heavy to lift.
I would say it was the coffin of a midget
Or a square baby
Were there not such a din in it.

The box is locked, it is dangerous.
I have to live with it overnight
And I can't keep away from it.
There are no windows, so I can't see what is in there.
There is only a little grid, no exit.

I put my eye to the grid.
It is dark, dark,
With the swarmy feeling of African hands
Minute and shrunk for export,
Black on black, angrily clambering.

How can I let them out?
It is the noise that appals me most of all,
The unintelligible syllables.
It is like a Roman mob,
Small, taken one by one, but my god, together!

I lay my ear to furious Latin.
I am not a Caesar.
I have simply ordered a box of maniacs.
They can be sent back.
They can die, I need feed them nothing, I am the owner.

I wonder how hungry they are.
I wonder if they would forget me
If I just undid the locks and stood back and turned into
    a tree.

There is the laburnum, its blond colonnades,
And the petticoats of the cherry.

They might ignore me immediately
In my moon suit and funeral veil.
I am no source of honey
So why should they turn on me?
Tomorrow I will be sweet God, I will set them free.

The box is only temporary.

Looking down into deep, still, clear pools of water, one sees the creatures slowly swimming upward. This is the land of Richard Cory, the land of wonder for what the box may contain; this is Ross Macdonald country. We carry within us the wonders we seek without us: there is all Africa and her prodigies in us. This is Sir Thomas Browne. As violence rises around us, as we drive those tacky California and Florida freeways of the modern condition, we find one of James's apertures upon the world opening before us in the modern crime story.

3

BUT THEN, even as children we all knew that people speak in two or more voices, that subtexts abound, that body language tells us as much as spoken language may do, and that appearances are deceiving.

Such discoveries are scarcely unique to detective fiction and they cannot account for the specific qualities of that fiction, or the unique *frisson* that readers attuned to the expectation of duplicity receive from it. The distance from Sylvia Plath's maniac bees to Yeats's bee-loud glade is enormous, one menacing and one warming, and yet both poems operate at several levels at which they meet. The simple presence of multiplicity is not enough to set mystery fiction apart from other fiction.

Of course, that is in part my point. For reasons not fully explicable, there are readers who are angered by the ambivalences of mystery fiction but who at once take pleasure from the ambivalences of Melville. Like all children, I had a father who lied to me on occasion, no doubt for what he thought was my own good, and if at times I was puzzled at the discovery of the fact, I cannot bring myself to respect him less for it. That he outwardly embraced religion, and inwardly doubted, represented a kind of truth I usefully learned early on, and this truth was easily compatible with the natural schizophrenia of the watcher-without and of the historian, who, while as a private person he is committed to political or social goals, must not allow those goals to dictate his views of the past he is reconstructing.

The question is, in part, a matter of degree; in part, a matter of levels of honesty (as opposed to mere trickery); and perhaps, in part, a matter of pride. My father could remind me of the religious meanings of Christmas, for he thought it right that I should not think of the day as one grand potlatch, my personal Indians descending from some remote giver of all consumer goodies to pay homage to my alleged goodness. So he never played games about Santa Claus, in whom I never believed, nor warned me that this strange apple-cheeked figure would not come down our chimney if I didn't behave. He made it clear that gifts were symbols of love, between us as a family, and that the world has chosen this annual occasion for us to restate this love because of a broader love for, and exchange of gifts with, a figure always referred to in our home somewhat remotely as "the Christ" (never in the familiar, as "Jesus"). All this seemed clear to me then and does now. Yet my father could also make a rather special point of Easter, to the extent that I was distraught to discover one day that the Easter Bunny was a myth, most probably because he had seemed a natural way to account for both the levity and the hint of anger that my father brought to discussions of the significance of Easter. While others were telling me tales of miraculous acts of ascension, he customarily brought Easter down to a level I could comprehend with a series of pointed (though bad) hot-crossed puns. So I didn't really expect anything to be as those around me said it would be, and I expected that matters would even seem more different to me than to others.

Then there was the day when my father suggested that I might enjoy reading some of the boys' books written by one Joseph Altsheler. He had enjoyed these books himself as a teenager, and one does like to pass on one's taste to others as a hedge against mortality, so he brought me some from the local library. Among his many books Altsheler had written a series about the Civil War. He took his reader directly into battle, at Shiloh or Gettysburg or Cross Keys, through the eyes of two protagonists, one young boy from the North and another from the South. Both Billy Yank and Johnny Reb were endowed with qualities of bravery and realistic fear, both came from sympathetic backgrounds, and both were proud of what they were fighting for. I devoured all these books, taking a basically pro-Northern sympathy—for I had been told that the Civil War was fought to free the slaves, and even now I know this to be so—into battle with me. My father had his prejudices, as we all do, but there was never a hint of racial bias in anything he ever said to me, and I presumed that the Southern case hadn't a leg to stand on. Yet here was an author I enjoyed, who, having allied me to him by saying all that I assumed to be true about Billy Yank, was now making Johnny Reb no less attractive a human being. A cynic might suggest that Altsheler was simply assuring his market throughout the country, not cutting himself off from any one region, but I think otherwise: I think he was a natural historian and a skillful detective. What he did was to show the same event—Stones River, let us say—through the eyes of two opposed figures. At some point in each novel the two young men, moving on quite separate paths to separate destinies, would appear within the same scene of action, not confronting each other directly, each indeed not even aware of the presence of the other. Carefully Altsheler then showed the event experienced in common through the partial facts as known to or seen by the individual participants. Here was interrogation of events at its best.

The juxtaposition of these books, possessed at manic speed rather than merely read, devoured in sequence so that one could see the entire War Between the States opening before one, had a profound effect on me. I discovered that there were no such things as exact facts but merely perceptions of those facts, and that what we generally regarded as "the facts, ma'am" was determined by who wrote the history—that is, most often by the victor. There was no single meaning to the bloody events that transpired at Pickett's Charge: there were two broadly assimilable meanings with the force of operable truths, and more discursively there were as many meanings as there were participants. Altsheler had done what no author of a school history text

[25]

had done for me: made me passionately interested in history, in the sense of wanting to know what people believed to be true, and why they believed in their particular visions of truth. From that time on, I pursued all fiction, whether in books or on the still-silver screen, that provided diverse apertures simultaneously upon my world. *Rashomon*, of course. Lawrence Durrell and his Alexandria Quartet, most certainly (though Altsheler was better). Paul Scott and his Raj Quarter, which closes in on the rape of a European woman in India at the moment of Indian independence, to see that act of violence, and the larger act for which it was metaphor, from the perspectives of four participants, each representative of a larger view (and here, at last, was a writer even better than Altsheler). Each of these interrogations of reality, met at different ages, made me more aware that people do not tell lies so much as reveal different truths, and in the gaps between these truths we, the listeners, make the lies.

Here, then, was one element central to a love for detective fiction: finding out what happened in terms of the many possible versions of events, through the many apertures upon what, given that each of us has but a single aperture through which to look, must be a House of Fiction even when we think it a House of History. But Altsheler suggested other possibilities as well. He was compassionate toward his figures, yet distant. He did not think that to criticize was to betray. He showed that the weak had great power over the strong. He was clear on the differences between guile, cunning, and deceit; he knew that, with the best intentions in the world through which we might walk aglittering, we nonetheless would likely tell the truth slant. This did not mean that he warned his readers not to trust people; quite the contrary, he told them that they should listen very carefully to precisely what people say (in all the ways in which things are "said"); moreover, he told them to trust the exact truth, the discrete fact, and to recognize that the lie arises from one's perception of the meaning to be attached to that truth or the connection to be made between one and another discrete fact. He brings us back to Roger Ackroyd.

Two other annoyingly autobiographical thoughts obtrude, before distance can enter this inquiry. The first has to do with the perception of justice. As a child growing up in the Middle and the Rocky Mountain West, one part of my sense of what justice meant came from an overdose of B-level Western motion pictures. Few of my generation do not remember Gene Autry (and a wee bit later, Roy Rogers, who seemed to be a usurper with his silly horse that did tricks rather than riding hard and straight) or, perhaps, the many obscure heroes who performed for Monogram Films. There was Hopalong Cassidy, of course, and Tom Mix, by then passing over the horizon, and just within my memory the last film of William S. Hart. John Wayne had begun in *Stagecoach* his long alliance with John Ford, but those of us who went to the Saturday morning matinees, partially because our parents wanted another addition to the set of dishes they were building up in those depression years, thought Wayne and Ford entirely too arty. We wanted those recognizable studio backgrounds, or the false fronts up the Kern River Canyon, and none of those Monument Valley sunsets that distracted the attention. We also needed our weekly fix: a little clean violence, some feathers-and-bows romance, and the sure knowledge that the white hats would beat the black hats in the end.

Then one day my parents left me off to see what, from the stills illuminated far below the markee (printer: no nonsense about *marquee;* this was in Colorado), was a conventional Western: *The Ox-Bow Incident.* Henry Fonda and Dana Andrews were a bit rich for my blood, but blood can thicken and it did. I sat alone, transfixed, in the balcony of a movie house in those long-ago days when a young boy needn't fear molestation, terrorist attack, or even a primal scene in the row ahead of him. A lynch mob took innocent people. Tension mounted, though a box of popcorn and one's moral sense of what was right (as well as all that conditioning by Gene Autry, who if he would only come along and break into "Springtime in the Rockies" would ease the tension) left one anticipating an unusually complex solution by which justice would be done. Of course, as all who have read the book or seen the film will know, justice was not done, and the innocent men were hanged.

As those ropes snapped tight a trapdoor opened beneath me. I did not yet know that evil sometimes is triumphant. I vomited in the aisle and, when met by my parents (free cup and saucer forgotten), asked to be put to bed. I stayed there three days. The doctor, I am told, diagnosed "brain fever," a convenient term when one doesn't know what is at the root of the evil, and he was not far from wrong. Later, when I came upon Melville's line about how little Pip, overboard and brain-dead, perceived that God goes a-blackberrying amongst the worlds, I felt confirmed. Some wear suits or white dresses to their confirmations; I simply came dressed in an odor of apprehension. Later, after reading *Moby Dick*, I summoned up the courage to return to Walter van Tilburg Clark, to read *The Track of the Cat*, and to discover—at least as I believe it—that he had written for the mountain West a direct parallel to Melville's excursion into the heart of darkness.

The other incident occurred rather later. I loved to read but I did not, aged about fourteen, love either *Silas Marner* or *Julius Caesar*. I would be a college student before I discovered the numbing, shaking solitudes by which *Hamlet* enriched me, and I would be an adult, in my early thirties, before I could bring myself to read George Eliot again. I remain convinced that it is better for children to be reading that which the world brands trash than not reading at all, and certain that with literature one must not run before one walks. A teacher found me in study hall, a copy of a now-forgotten paperback entitled *I Wake Up Screaming* hidden somewhere in Raveloe amidst the linen-weavers. The book was torn in half before my eyes, deposited with dramatic disgust in a nearby wastebasket, surrogate sewer, and the entire assemblage was informed that my taste was despicable. Had I been caught reading *Hustler* in a nunnery, I could not have been the object of greater loathing (or more intense fascination). Happily my family moved some weeks later to another state and I was able to leave the outward signs of my perversion to the long passage of two-lane asphalt that separated one state of reality from another. In a sense I was fortunate, for I read almost nothing thereafter, devoting the next year to the unbookish pursuits thought more appropriate by my teachers and my community: girls, sex, the Boy Scouts, and athletics, in which I excelled by running around a quarter mile of cinder track more rapidly than nearly anyone else, an accomplishment that brought in train triumph in those related endeavors. And eventually, Eagle Scout badge and three palms on my chest, virginity presumed lost, society's definitions of success achieved, I could by my last year in high school begin to read once again. The book I started with was Alan Paton's *Cry, the Beloved Country*, and by so small a margin of choice did old interests, Altsheler and *The Hound of the Baskervilles* (read while hiding under a dining room table, alone in a house on a thunderous night, nearly eight years before), justice and cowboy movies, history and detective stories, lead me to college and the study of a British Empire from which Doyle, and Paton, and those Boy Scouts all sprang.

Of course, I could, by then, sense why so tawdry a title, packaged with simulated rape scene on cover and erective description on back, as *I Wake Up Screaming* should have so angered a teacher who thought she had detected higher thoughts in my teenage head. I also understood that there is great literature, of which society approves, and literature that is not great. I understood that I had no right to reject society's definitions of great literature until I had met it on its own plateau of greatness. Years later, as an adult, when walking through the Altepinakothek in Munich, smothered by the undulating pink flesh of Rubens upon Rubens, I suddenly realized that, college courses notwithstanding, I was not required to believe Rubens a great artist, much less like him, and with a sense of falling free I knew that thereafter I would read, write, drink, and do what my own taste told me I must. That a man should be past thirty before deciding that a character—his character —should be (William Gass speaking) the noise of his own name, the sounds and rhythms that proceed from him and not to him, is a statement about education and family and perhaps America; it is certainly a statement about literature.

Yet that sense of distance from others remains, is deepened by the sense of closeness to oneself. Events, facts, must still flow by as though on an excursion, the scenery from which we fashion a perception of reality. We pass through our environment as on a train, travelers, fascinated, pleased, excited, more exalted by the journey than by the destination. These are the characteristics that describe mystery fiction: if the journey is seen as a cheat, if there is no pleasure in being fooled and fairly, if one cannot find within the underliterature the mirror of the overliterature, then one, it seemed to me, had no grasp on society as a whole, no sense of the sociology of knowledge, no self.

4

STILL, IT *is* a battle to "take seriously" (a phrase itself worth a Gass on being blue) detective fiction, a battle made the more desperate by the obvious fact that so many practitioners of the craft think it best not to take their own such fiction seriously. One of the most insidious, aware paragraphs Graham Greene has ever written has always seemed to me to be this one, which begins as a reply to a question put to a waitress as to whether a woman, Else, an apparent suicide, had been the one to tell the waitress that she had been living with a married man in Highbury: "Did *she* tell you that?"

"Oh no. She was a quiet one. But you pick up things." He watched her with horror: this was friendship. He watched the small brown heartless eyes while she invented things even as she talked. There wasn't a man at Highbury except in that romantic and squalid brain. Was it she who had lent Else those novelettes which had conditioned her speech? She said, "I think it was the children was the difficulty." There was a kind of gusto of creation in the voice. Else was safely dead; she could be reconstructed now to suit anybody at all. . . .

The line between friendship and manipulation is an easy one. All great art is manipulative, and those who are on friendly terms with the arts may expect to be manipulated. One might object that one so Philistine as to be pushed to self-awareness by a bad writer of crude boys' books, by the tension between silly and serious Western films, or by a teacher's overreaction to trashy lit (or who had to wait to see Rubens in all his flesh on the wall rather than handsomely reproduced in a more accessible classroom book before knowing what he thought) is utterly doomed to measure quality in the crudest terms. And one who thinks Greene's "entertainments" superior to his "more serious work" (the latter phrase is Greene's publisher's terminology) would obviously prefer to bed down with Harriet Vane rather than with Tess of the d'Urbervilles. But before concluding this, we might ask why a master of duplicity should be taken at face value when he appears to be downgrading his "entertainments" below his "more serious work," and why, even if Greene here is at his ironic and self-mocking best, so many writers of superior mystery and detective fiction apparently feel (or their publisher feels for them) that their books must bear the subtitle *A Novel*. Is "a novel" by definition superior to "a thriller"? The apparent answer is yes, since thrillers always, and detective "novels" often (despite hiding behind the protective coloration of the notion of "the novel"), still ride at the back of the bus, segregated out for special, often trite, review columns in the *New York Times Book Review*, or the *Times Literary Supplement*, or *The New Republic*. Second-class status is written plain on the face of these columns, where nine hundred words may be devoted to five or six mystery novels and, on the adjacent pages, two thousand words to the latest inquiry into the mating instincts of the bee. Sylvia Plath would have been pleased.*

Many academicians have written mystery stories under pseudonyms, often (they say) because they fear that their more serious work would be compromised or undervalued if it were widely known that they also indulge in a bit of pleasure from time to time. This is rather like suggesting that the author of a standard text in biology would lose credentials were it known that he kept a mistress on the side. Carolyn Heilbrun, for example, did not reveal to her colleagues in the Department of English at Columbia University that she was also Amanda Cross until she was voted tenure. This compromise must still rankle, since her most recent book, *Death in a Tenured Position*, is her best, angriest, most pointed. Carolyn Heilbrun is a distinguished scholar. She has written an authoritative and utterly compelling book on the theme of androgyny in literature. She has pursued the Bloomsbury group. She has written one of

* For some years I have been writing a review column, simply labeled "Mysteries," for *The New Republic*. Once upon a time a review editor let me write to whatever length seemed necessary, even to the point of developing entire essays on P. D. James, William Haggard, Robert Duncan, and Donald Hamilton. Literary editors come and go. One suggested that no one of good judgment "except his wife" ever read detective fiction, and he wondered why I did. The column soon dropped to nine hundred words. A literary editor of a different journal remarked that his readers were in pursuit of serious matters; perhaps so, though shortly before he had given over a page to Gore Vidal's *Myra Breckinridge*, a farrago of nonsense, and soon after two pages were surrendered to a so-called work of history by a man who has been writing for years that Adolf Hitler had no idea that Jews were being killed in Germany. Of course, we all have different mirrors to hold up to life and some can get pretty steamy. Still, one wonders about those mirrors that reveal no breath of life whatever.

the best essays ever written on Dorothy Sayers, whom she takes seriously.* She is, I think, a highly skilled novelist of manners in an academic setting, and she has chosen the device of the mystery because she enjoys it, because she admires Sayers, and because she saw earlier than many that behind the alleged snobbery of Miss Sayers is a deeply committed feminism. If one reads *Gaudy Night* today—one of Dorothy Sayers's three best books by a good margin—one can scarcely comprehend the condescending remark of the usually perceptive Jacques Barzun and Wendell Taylor, that the book suffers from a "combination of gossip and 'outrages,' " which are dismissed as "merely vandalism and attempts to frighten." That is, no one is murdered. In the meantime, Miss Sayers gives us one of the angriest, most chilling denunciations of a university utterly dominated by men that one can find. I have never read an angrier feminist novel, and the dismissive note by Barzun and Taylor in their formidably valuable *Catalogue of Crime*, that while "the don-esses are sometimes hard to keep apart, the architecture is very good," is simply—no, complexly—silly.

Carolyn Heilbrun, then, writing as Amanda Cross, is "the American Sayers." Her novels are not so intricately plotted (none could be so wastefully intricate as *The Five Red Herrings*, vapidly retitled for its American audience *Suspicious Characters*, which turns upon the improbable proposition [today] that trains run precisely to schedule). The actual mystery involved is usually relatively transparent. Yet to think of an Amanda Cross novel as "the bookish woman's Harlequin Romance" (as one reviewer remarked) is the ultimate insult, unless one does accept Kant's dictum

---

* Heilbrun, "Sayers, Lord Peter and God," *American Scholar*, XXXVII (Spring, 1968), 324–34.

that a sufficient difference in degree becomes a difference in kind.

Sayers wanted all her life to be a don, and she lived on the fringes of Oxbridge academic life, turning increasingly to Christian apologetics and, in "Are Women Human?," to the muted anger of advocacy for a cause. Carolyn Heilbrun has, in her own right and in her persona as Amanda Cross, achieved that which Sayers wanted. In her most recent work of scholarship Heilbrun examines the problems of *Inventing Womanhood*. The pendulum then swings, for she has alternated her "serious work" with her "novels," to *Death in a Tenured Position*. This metronomic rhythm seems utterly satisfying to author and reader alike. It produces works of great civility, insight, and cleverness, and with a single exception (*The Question of Max*), of genuine literary merit. The academic figures in Amanda Cross's books all speak well, wittily, with quotations from the great authors as ready ripostes in all situations; the air of life in a grand Senior Common Room is beguiling. She has been criticized for showing us academics as they wish they spoke rather than as they truly speak, but surely this too is of the artifice of art; do any of us imagine that King Lear spoke to his daughters precisely as Shakespeare tells us? Both give us language as it ought to be spoken, and Amanda Cross is as full of wry, quotable lines as are the novelists and poets her heroes and villains quote. The comedy of manners, which flourished with Sayers, has found an American home with Amanda Cross. There is no real mystery to *The James Joyce Murders*, though there is much pleasure and high good sense.

Why, then, does so good a writer also label her books "a novel"? Why did she think it necessary to hide her loathsome vice from her colleagues until, in a tenured position, she could take the Rubens down from the wall?

Why do so many professors, the very guardians of our literary traditions, hide behind pseudonyms? For they do. There is the English tradition: C. Day Lewis, a poet laureate, who was Nicholas Blake; J.I.M. Stewart, Reader in English at Oxford, who is Michael Innes; and any number of doctors (Jonathan Gash), solicitors (Michael Gilbert), ex-colonial officials (William Haggard), and ex-diplomats (John le Carré) who take on new personas when they set out to "merely entertain." Would one say *"merely connect"* in just such a tone of voice?

The need to hide one's commitment to underliterature is not peculiar to Britain. Hubert Monteilhet (*Murder at the Frankfurt Book Fair*) is a professor in the Sorbonne. Robert B. Parker began writing his Spenser novels while a professor in the Boston area, and the ties between his series figure and Spenserian attitudes were clear to anyone who had ever worried about *The Faerie Queene*. Tony Hillerman, who teaches journalism at the University of New Mexico, has created Joe Leaphorn, Navajo policeman, and guides his readers adroitly through Navajo cosmology as an integral part of his plots. Trevanian, of *The Eiger Sanction, The Loo Sanction, The Main* (set in Montreal), and *Shibumi* is a former academic who obviously takes pleasure in confusing reviewers. Stephen Greenleaf, a law professor, and James K. MacDougall, a professor of English, have written superior crime fiction. One trusts they have, or will get, tenure. And in England again, it is common for teachers in the public schools and colleges of education to write detective fiction on the side: William McIllvanney and Colin Dexter are among the best. "Straight" novelists have written detective fiction, of course: Kingsley Amis, William Faulkner, Ernest Hemingway, and (as I would classify the mystery) Willa Cather in the Outland sequence to *The Professor's House*. But we usually dismiss these as aberrations, experiments, though had *Intruder in the Dust* been written by Richard North Patterson rather than William Faulkner it too would have taken its seat at the back of the bus.

Obviously worms are at work here. There is more to the question than mere snobbery, and more than the willingness of such writers to hide their detective fiction behind fictitious names or to dismiss it as "an entertainment." There is more to the problem than the fact that murder mysteries deal with murder, and crime fiction with crime, and some little old ladies in those well-worn tennis shoes do not care to read about either (though I have never met a little old lady who didn't like Allingham, Christie, Marsh, and more recently P. D. James—another pseudonym, that, though Phyllis White has come out from hiding—or Robert Barnard, Sheila Radley, and June Thomson, to name three new trees erect on the horizon). Something more is at work than the sense of guilt in the reader, and especially the academic reader, that forces one to dismiss detective fiction as simple relaxation, as though one were at a bit of golf or taking an evening off for beer and skittles. There is something more at work than the fear of being thought mediocre —to read literature deemed mediocre, to drive a car, drink wine, listen to music that lacks class—in taste and thus in performance. There is something more at work than a perverse and imperfect Gresham's law, by which a mud flow of truly bad, sensational, sexually explicit, masochistic fiction sits cheek by pudenda with those who are giving us their private vision of hell, as the Dorothy Sayers who translated Dante did as surely as the Dorothy Sayers who rang the Nine Tailors also did. There is something more at work than the fear that detective fiction belongs to the masses, or that it sustains its life through the paperback, in drugstores, newsstands, and airport gift shops. More is at work than relatively small print runs, short shelf life, and teachers who rip books in half. Though all these matters are involved, of course, one must look elsewhere for an explanation of why the special joys of detective fiction should fail to attract more "serious" attention.

One prime reason may be that a goodly number of such books are badly written. But then so too are an equally goodly number of "straight" novels. If C. P. Snow usually wrote well (and he did), so did B. Traven. Both also wrote badly at times. If Robert Louis Stevenson wrote well, so does Geoffrey Household.

Another prime reason may be that detective fiction is a relatively inflexible genre, often with a form as precise as that of a sonnet. Not everyone likes sonnets either. Even if one does, Shakespeare comes only once a generation, if that.

Another reason may be that, in the world of modern commerce—and detective fiction grew in and out of that world, springing from the thirst for apparent scientific accuracy, from the need to see a rational world behind the chaos of the industrial revolution—the writer must write what will sell. Having found his audience, many an author tends then to write for that audience to assure a continued income. Formulaic fiction also becomes formulaic style, the package as before, dependable, without artistic growth or experimentation. Thus died Ian Fleming, victimized by the great success of James Bond, and thus may pass Ross Macdonald, acute, clever, and fixed in space and time. The author becomes trapped in a box of his own making. Those like Len Deighton, le Carré, Arthur Conan Doyle, who have tried to break from the box, have found that the great public, the people, are a mob, sir! and will not tolerate deviation.

Another reason may be that detective and mystery fiction adapt poorly to the screen or stage and hardly at all to television, so that authors and books are less reinforced than they are destroyed by modern communications. Part of the mystery in any thriller arises from the ambiguity of the words; since in film the only ambiguity that can dependably be transmitted arises from what one sees, a different style is required. One begins to write to a visual intent. How could one effectively translate those key passages from *The Murder of Roger Ackroyd* into visual terms without cheating? What we see is less frightening than what we imagine. Anyone frightened by seeing Stanley Kubrick's *Shining* wished devoutly to be frightened; anyone left unfrightened by H. F. Heard's *Taste of Honey* has never been in a bee-loud glade, much less held the swarm of a continent in his hands. The only successful transfer of detective fiction to film was made in the early years of television when Raymond Burr's Perry Mason became more real than Erle Stanley Gardner's version. One can no more transfer Rex Stout's Nero Wolfe to the screen than one could give us the Winnie-the-Pooh and Piglet of our childhood.

Perhaps the most important reason why detective fiction has not attracted more serious attention is that it frightens many people. Icicles in the eye hurt.

An interesting question, as one views the world's fictions, is why the British detective writer so often interposes a Watson or Hastings figure between the detective and the reader. The most obvious answer, of course, is that Doyle needed the brave, slow-thinking Watson for Holmes to offer up explanations to, in order to get through great gobs of explanatory material that otherwise would have had to be written inside a cartoonist's balloon, as though Holmes were thinking to himself. This removes the icicle, as well as the mote, from the eye of the one to that of the other. Miss Christie's Hercule Poirot needed Hastings for the same reason, and also to bring in the soothing sense of a sound

Briton standing behind the rather irritating and very foreign little Belgian. Yet this answer is insufficient, for surely conventional drawing room detective fiction as written in the United States had to get through explanatory material as well.

But then it does, someone might say: Ellery Queen has his father, the Inspector, to try his ideas out on, and Mr. and Mrs. North had each other. True enough, though the general lack of the Watson/Hastings figure in American detective fiction is worth remarking upon. Perhaps the lack arises from the American preference for the loner, who works as an utter individualist within and sometimes against the grain of society. Perhaps the pervasive American dislike for the policeman provides a better foil than Watson or Hastings could be, likable and woolly minded as they are, for our individualistic, sometimes amateur, lone detective is able in the end to make fools of the police, showing that men who work within organizations are less free to think creatively in resolving puzzles. My own guess is that the strongest reason why the amanuensis (Archie Goodwin notwithstanding) is so rare in American fiction is that the sentimental streak in Spade, Marlowe, and Archer requires that they be their own Watson or Hastings: that they interrogate themselves in their search for an identity.

American and British crime fiction, and indeed that of Western Europe in general, is set apart from crime fiction in Eastern Europe, or in dictatorships generally (here one includes, until quite recently, Spain and Portugal, where detective writers hardly exist), by a different set of concerns—though a set that at root may arise from the same division between man working with man (in British fiction, and in Dorothy Sayers, for which read man working with woman) and man working at odds with himself—that the debate over individualism has pretty well silenced. One must admit to crime before one may write of it, and this rules out the Soviet Union. One must concede man's imperfectibility, and at least admit to one's thought a variety of psychological theories that emphasize individual growth or distortion, before one can probe motive with a sense of wonder and variety, and this limits Marxist writers (though it does not rule them out). Crime literature is, despite its conservative conclusions, a literature arising from protest, from closely observing society and its ills, and unless a tradition of commenting on the ills of society is encouraged, detective fiction is not likely to be encouraged. Though the distance between Thoreau and Ross Macdonald may seem great to some readers, it is surely covered by a straight line.

Three authors, neither British nor American, best represent the ways in which one may circle around these approaches to life. Anglo-American writers such as Henry James or Anglo-Irish like Elizabeth Bowen were particularly attracted to how illusions were created and despoiled; they loved paradox, and even when coziest their tone was one of isolating irony. Akin to them, I am thinking of Georges Simenon, Belgian-born though usually taken for French, and the team of Swedish writers Maj Sjöwall and Per Wahlöö. Here are writers who set about showing us how to lose our innocence in ways that arise from society more than from human character, and to this extent they share the vaguely deterministic views of the anti-individualist school, while they are also clear that, because *Maigret Has Scruples* (1958) or a prostitute named Teresa (in Sjöwall and Wahlöö's *Laughing Policeman*) had limits, individual acts still count.

Simenon, like Graham Greene, consciously divided his work into entertainments—the conventional Maigret stories —and into psychological novels. The gap between these is, I think, less self-conscious and also less successful than in

Greene's work, for both types of books are concerned with a single set of questions: Who does society appoint to ask its questions for it? How does society deal with the answers when they are unpleasant? By creating a series figure both Simenon and the Swedish team do something Greene cannot do, however: they show how a Maigret or a Martin Beck is slowly worn down by the rôle of grand inquisitor, diminished, made tired of society itself. When the protagonist is a series figure, he is able to grow, to develop from book to book, and provided the author is concerned with life and not pasteboard (as in Fleming's James Bond), age brings exhaustion, boredom, the loss of illusions. In this way, their series figures actually grow as they diminish, for they become more real for becoming less heroic. Simenon's quiet, deadpan observation of repetitively wet French nights is not to everyone's taste—I confess to having really liked only five or six of the books from his enormous output, and that I rather conventionally agree that *The Man Who Watched the Trains Go By* (one of the psychological thrillers, superbly translated by Stuart Gilbert) is his best —just as Martin Beck's stomach problems, decaying marriage, and blandly unattractive daughter do not grow on one from book to book. Yet in the one, an understanding of why crime is always with us, French style, and in the other, a sharper, ultimately angrier statement about how government must corrupt, Swedish style, provide two valuable and sustained critiques of modern life as lived in the West, by writers who would not, their critical views to the contrary, care to live in Dostoevski's Russia.

Simenon raises another question. He produced well over two hundred books, some in three or four days; such productivity led many critics to dismiss him as an autodidact. In general it is true that his Maigret stories are less compelling than the psychological novels that won him great praise from André Gide and others, though there is no firm evidence that he took longer to write the psychological novels. One suspects, rather, that as an author takes on a different persona, his perception of the intended audience rightly changes, with substantially different results. The best case in point is John Creasey, English author of over six hundred books under at least twenty-eight pseudonyms. As J. J. Marric he created the well-crafted, usually compelling Gideon series; as Jeremy York he wrote a vapid series about Superintendent Folly; his Toff series is execrable; his Roger West books, written as Creasey, are formulaic and dependably entertaining. One approach seems not to have carried over into another, each formula having been worked out and adhered to with intelligence and care.

Thus the close reader of detective fiction is presented with a special problem when a friend asks for a recommendation of "a good mystery to read on the flight." One must know the friend extremely well to comprehend the question. One must know whether the series figure if there be one—Maigret, Beck, Donald Hamilton's Matt Helm—will be pleasant company. One must know the friend's politics, his ear for language, his sense of order and disorder, his favorite country, and the nature of his particular innocence. One knows few people so well. Good friends do not ask serious readers of detective fiction to recommend something they will like.

Thus as entertainment detective fiction is not, cannot be, taken with true seriousness, for it appears to lack interchangeability: no two cultivated readers can agree on what is excellent. As it murmurs to us of our dreams, it reminds us of our failings, as individuals and as a society. Murmurings do not belong on film. Willa Cather knew something when, after the second disastrous filming of *A Lost Lady*, she left it in her will that none of her books was ever to be translated into a motion picture, television film, or any other visual medium that might in future be invented. In this unintelligible world, the burden of the mystery has become as much a matter of mood as of puzzle—as close to Wordsworth as to Poe. Our moods are visual. Except in rare instances—the Australian film *Breaker Morant* is one such instance—visual modes no longer successfully carry pure narrative. As narrative breaks down, all becomes mystery, of obscure origin, of obscure nature, of obscure purpose, hidden, secret. In seeking to follow the path to its conclusion, to learn about the mystery of the bloodstained tea cozy, those of us who take this path not chosen, watchers-without, cameras, distant, become beneficially released from a consciousness that, as a practical matter of daily living, tells us what is and is not. We change. We feel the ground under our feet. We think we know where we are. The moving is over and done. A different form of certitude arises: appearances deceive, but in the end the detectives that are our doubts resolve the contradictions, show that apparently irrational ends have rational causes, link event to event in meaningful patterns, and re-create a great chain of being that satisfies the deeply conservative need to believe that though we cannot perceive it or account for it, there is even yet order in the universe. Surely this hope we take with such true seriousness—as the historian seeks in the past the values others seek in churches, so the detective of fiction finds a higher justice than society can hope to create—that we fear to examine it too closely. For some, at least, the divisions of the rosary that correspond to the mysteries of redemption are best counted off on the beads of hidden, secret things, each bead a fact, a clue, to our environment.

And besides, reading detective fiction is fun.

5

I DEAS HAVE consequences. So do actions. Espionage novels, as they are somewhat archly called, illustrate these obvious truths more than gothic fiction (which sometimes contains no ideas) or traditional mystery fiction (where the element of trickery may overcome the element of logic, as in John Dickson Carr's sterile exercises in sophistry, sometimes called "locked-room puzzles"). Rational motivation or the presumption of it; that presumption linked to the study of character; a Burkean view of the human condition; Hannah Arendt's knowledge that the human condition includes the banality of evil; an interesting mental and moral landscape of fear across which to move the action; a perfectly felt location, a sense of place, a hard environment that influences the choice of actions and the consequential options: these are the ingredients of good spy or thriller fiction. The CIA, KGB, MI5, and the rest of the alphabet soup are simply the interchangeable actors on the stage. No subset of fiction within the genre can better illustrate how actions have consequences than spy fiction can.

No action should be without thought. Whack of ball, spin of wheel, lift of glass, angry word: each is to pull a trigger, and the professional doesn't point a gun unless he is prepared to use it, and he isn't prepared to use it unless the consequences are more desirable than other consequences are likely to be. Maturity means knowing there are options, having a sense of responsibility toward one's actions, thinking out the possible scenarios that might follow from opening this door, closing that one. This is the baroque mind at work. Science-fiction writers and the great cities encased in glass bubbles they create have scant tolerance for baroque buildings. One is told that the time came in the Company when James Angleton's interest in orchids was so baroque no one could tell what scenario he had in mind. That, of course, is the point.

I teach in a university customarily modified by the word *great*. This means that the students are treated as though they are more intelligent than most. Objective criteria suggest that they are. They also have very large egos, and so they put their ideas, their actions, first, with little thought for the consequences. To think through alternative scenarios requires sublimating the ego into another's, and most of us aren't very good at that. I also live on the campus of the great university, so I have more than my share of close encounters on the campus. One could write a weekly column about them.

Item: Five years or so ago I was run down by a student riding a bicycle going the wrong way on a one-way street. My mistake: I should have known to look both ways nonetheless. Why should the rules of the road apply to a busy graduate student anyway? The bike pinned me against the side of a car, broke three ribs; the rider fell to the ground, leapt up and took a quick look to see if I was breathing, shouted, "Sorry, sir" (it was the *sir* that told me he was a graduate student), and rode off again. The year before that I had been in an airplane, flying ground contact only from Delhi to Tashkent, and had made an emergency landing in a blizzard at Khandahar airport in Afghanistan. I passed three days sleeping fully dressed-and-booted in a freezing concrete bunker, without food. This might have been viewed as dangerous, though no ribs were broken. The year after my ribs were broken for me I was in an elevator in Chandigarh, viewing Le Corbusier's less

[46]

than grand new city, when the cable snapped and fourteen of us fell a floor or so. In school I had played football, some basketball, and had run hard at track. I had never had a broken bone until I stepped out in front of that graduate student.

Item: Three years later I broke two of the same ribs again: in the university library, working rapidly through the card catalogue, I rounded a hard corner at speed and struck a card tray, left extended by someone working even more urgently than I without time to slide the tray the twelve inches needed back to safety. A very few weeks before that I had stood on a street corner in Bucharest, unable to understand a word of the language around me, or even to find anyone who could comprehend my bad German, and I had felt a sense of joy, of breaking free, for there was no one with whom I could communicate, or was expected to communicate, or who could communicate with me. The university is a community, we say, where each looks out for the other: this means thinking of consequences. Bucharest was, for me, not a community, and there were no tie-lines out, no anchors, no connections to any discernible consequences.

Ideas mislead, of course, and that is a consequence too. Once, in Saigon, with wife and small daughter, I stayed in a hotel that had, a few weeks before, been invaded by terrorists. We arose in predawn dark to go to the airport and were turned back halfway there; the airport was closed, under some form of attack. We spent another day in the city, peaceful, sunny and yet surprisingly cool for May, though the month really meant relatively little save as between wet and not wet. That night, under mosquito netting, I heard someone move in the tiny cubicle that served as a shower stall and lavatory; the only ill-secured access to the room was through a tiny window from cubicle to hallway. A tiny Vietnamese-size figure scuttled out of the room; I looked to the adjacent bed for the form of my wife, saw her, and leapt upon the figure, shouting out, "Stop!" and seizing the creature around the throat. Brave act, quick thought, family saved. The figure was my wife, the figure in the bed, pillows; the transom still secured, my nightmare of expectation the reality on which I had acted. Being a sensible woman she immediately hit me in the ribs so that I let her loose. She didn't break them, though.

Actions have consequences. There can be no more prudential fiction than spy fiction, since it assumes that all actions have consequences that link, were we only able to see the links. Let us remain within the cozy confines of the campus one more time before going haring off across the Scottish hills. There is, in a great university library, an archive relating to the history of that great university. Historians and librarians together being pack rats and moles, even accession records for library books dating from the 1940s have been kept. Were one to be going through these accession records in quest of God knows what and I won't tell, one might casually observe that throughout World War II, even in 1944, German scholarly journals continued to be received. It boggles the mind to think of those scholars, burrowing away under the rubble in the cities of Germany, still producing their papers on Goethe, or the effects of Zyclon-B gas on rabbits. It boggles the mind to think of how those scholarly journals got printed; how they got delivered to the United States; how they found their way to the shelves of a great university library. That is a few too many boggles.

And so the original query is set aside to follow a different hare to its hole. How did those journals reach those shelves? Well, they came from Switzerland. How were they paid for? Well, money was sent to Istanbul. It says so, right here in the records. Then where, in fact, are the journals? Well, they were transferred years ago. And where is the man who processed the orders? Dead. And the man who authorized the expenditures? Alive and well, but he couldn't tell you anything; he wasn't here—everyone knows he spent the entire war in London. Who, precisely, paid for these journals that can't be found? A bank in New York. Who signed the checks? Will Mystery to Mathematics fly? (that's Pope); why this damnable demand for exactitude? (And so began the book I am writing next.)

The basic premise of good thriller or spy fiction is founded upon just such trivia. The unobserved detail is the important detail. All detail must be observed. There is always more detail. The horizon recedes infinitely. This creates joy.

The basic formula for spy fiction was laid down by John Buchan, master of the Scottish landscape. One takes an attractive hero, slightly introspective though not debilitatingly so, that we might look just a little way down into the clear pool. One endows this hero with some special expertise acquired in some remote place: Richard Hannay is a white from southern Africa, who learned from the natives how to throw a knife into the air and catch it between his teeth, a man who moved quietly through the bush and who knew just where, behind the right ear and just low enough toward the shoulder blade, to press in order to render a man silently unconscious. One places this hero in an environment in which he is less comfortable, one we ordinarily would call civilized, where his animal instincts and natural goodness are muted. London will do. One then plunges him, by accident (as in *The Thirty-Nine Steps*) or design (as in *Greenmantle*), into a perilous situation.

Unlike mystery fiction, spy fiction adjusts to the motion-picture screen superlatively well, and no one ever did it better than Alfred Hitchcock, even when he changed utterly Buchan's own book. To *The Thirty-Nine Steps* Hitchcock added what he called a MacGuffin—a word he stuck with through all his pictures. A MacGuffin is visually essential; on the printed page it is valuable though not indispensable. When asked what a MacGuffin was, Hitchcock replied with a classic shaggy-dog story. Two passengers, one English and one Scottish, are on a train in Scotland. The Englishman, noticing a large, oddly shaped and wrapped parcel on the luggage rack above, asks the Scot what it is. "It's a MacGuffin." "What is a MacGuffin?" "It's for trapping lions in the Highlands." Without thought of consequence, the Englishman declares, "But there are no lions in the Highlands." "Well, then, there are no MacGuffins." (Hitchcock, in his version, didn't identify which was Scot and which Englishman, though John Buchan would have known.) So one brings in the red herring, the diversion, the hound with which the hare will run. One may now double-cross anyone.

Now the classic spy story has nearly taken shape, though there are still two pieces of the structure that are essential. The hero must be given a task to perform—to find the Bruce-Partington plans, to stop the sinister figure in the trench coat from getting onto the balcony below which the Queen will pass, to carry a secret message the meaning of which he does not know himself from place x to place y; indeed, to get from x to y without knowing that he has a secret message on him, secreted in the middle cigarette in his silver case. (The agent who slipped the message in there knows that the cigarette will not be smoked, because ten minutes before, in the bar over a gin and tonic, he heard our hero say that he had sworn off smoking, and since he is a hero, we and the agent can count on his resolve to do precisely as he promised. Our hero, having promises to keep, will go miles before he sleeps.) There must be opposition to the performance of the task; failure to complete the task must mean the destruction of all civilization, or at least of the British Empire, which is much the same thing; and while the consequences of failure to complete the task must be clear—that destruction of civilization— the consequences of completing it must be vaguely unclear, to leave room for the MacGuffin to work its way in the end.

The opposition must come from two directions, so that we may wait to see our hero blind-sided. The enemy must be in pursuit, of course, and they will seldom be hampered by any questions of fair play or side issues of ancillary consequences to innocent parties. But the natural allies of the hero must also be in pursuit, or at least actively un-cooperative, lest he simply go to the police with his problem and dump it into their dull procedural laps. So the spy, amateur or professional, must move alone, all society set against him, perhaps even his own control betraying him. He is a figure out of *High Noon*, standing tall against the sky, protecting society against itself as it becomes ever more entrammeled in its rituals of civilization, hiding behind rules that do not apply out there on the prairie, on the pampas, in the jungle, when being pursued. With two groups in pursuit, our hero (and we the reader) can never be entirely certain whether the attractive young lady who by inadvertence falls into the story is a plant by one group or the other, a *belle dame sans merci*, or merely a *deus ex machina* by which our hero, discovering that he cannot live for himself alone, elevates his raw, low cunning into true imaginative courage, and having taken her into danger with him, rescues both at the last moment.

"At the last moment": this is the other essential element of the structure. There must be a time constraint on the action, a ticking time bomb, a countdown by which pursuit, delay, movement are measured in absolute terms. Each second must count, though it must be seen in the larger context of the final deadline. Without a timetable, one cannot know how late it is.

These elements in hand, they must be fitted to a landscape, for spy fiction is cinematic, visual, the sense of place providing a good measure of the sense of menace. Graham Greene was a master at this; so, in fact, and for other purposes, are Anthony Burgess and Lawrence Durrell. The hero survives in the end because he is more elemental, better able to use the landscape to his advantage. The enemy, aliens in fact or in spirit, do not know how to go to ground. The earth in its neutrality, its indifference, is not in the end malevolent; it is, as in Stephen Crane's "Open Boat," indifferently rewarding the person closest to it, whose land it is. One can smell the heather and feel the winds and icy mountain streams in John Buchan, and one knows that down in the glens the pursuers will be just a bit more chilled than Richard Hannay. The hero is at home in his environment, and because at home, he can quickly find his way even in an environment utterly unknown to him; he knows how to read the maps; the landscapes of fear produce a healthy tension under which he acts while the pursuers, though creators of the action by virtue of their pursuit, are actually reacting. Those swarms of bees are, to the beekeeper, friends.

This, then, is the formula. Though overlaid with convolutions extreme, sex explicit, and place-names unpronounceable, the formula today beneath the new cover is little changed. Perhaps, in truth, the formula began with Rudyard Kipling, who in *Kim* provided nearly all of the elements, and certainly the structure, the setting. It was Kipling who referred to spying as the Great Game, especially in the context of holding the Russians, over the Northwest Frontier from India, at bay. Reread today, *Kim* has all these elements and more, but it is a poor primer to the genre, for a first reading today is marred by the static that arises from his apparent condescension, from what some readers—deeply mistaken—take to be racism, and from its frequent, authentic, and confusing use of Anglo-Indian wallah words. Read after one has felt one's way into the genre, read at leisure in a hotel in Lahore, looking out on the great gun Zam-Zam with which the book's descriptive passage begins, *Kim* may be seen for the masterpiece it is.

This excursus on Kipling is meant to bootleg two additional problems to the reader. One is that the rules of the Great Game have changed, and so has the temper of spy fiction. Today one may vomit into the aisle daily if disturbed by justice not being done, for while the formula is still at work, it is manipulated differently. There no longer is a dependable heroic type. Travis McGee, John D. MacDonald's presumably lovable beach bum, is a male chauvinist who still thinks that the best cure for a woman's blues is a good screw. James Bond, Ian Fleming's walking set of brand names, achieves his triumphs in the end solely because he has a superior technology at his fingertips. Smiley roots out the mole from among the honourable schoolboys at the cost of evasion, a marriage built on lies, and worst of all, the incapacity to trust anyone. Honor is for schoolboys. Buchan, Graham Greene, Eric Ambler, those early and mid-passage masters of the spy thriller, knew that violence, including moral violence, was best when both rationed and various. Today the hero kills almost by reflex, a survivor, ego up and card tray pulled out, aware yet unheedful of consequence. Hollow men litter the landscape, having reversed our moral expectations: once one walked among those filled with rebellion on the inside while showing complicity on the outside, the standard spy, standard betrayer, standard human being leading a life of quiet desperation. Today, in spy fiction, one is surrounded by those who show rebellion on the outside and are all complicity on the inside, supporting macho male bonding (Meyer and McGee), the inherent right of the State (Robin Moore), and either vigilante justice (Brian Garfield) or total paranoia (Robert Ludlum). No strong men standing against the horizon, these, but merely other bits of the human landscape who survive by playing the game. But playing the game is not the Great Game. In this change, we mirror society in its despairs, the hero gone, action now carried by the antihero, by that mechanical figure referred to by the critics as the protagonist, or worse yet, the interlocutor, by those who ask the questions or provide the unmotivated action that advances the narrative.

Of course, to reflect society properly it is right that we no longer assume that all virtue is on one side of the coin, the side that also says *E Pluribus Unum*. Samuel Johnson told us so in 1759, in *Rasselas*: "Inconsistencies cannot both be right, but imputed to man they may both be true." Properly enough we now have spy novels (and some histories) that prove Churchill the evil, and Hitler the noble, man; more that show the Americans to be at least as vicious as the Russians, and the prime movers as well; and a spate of tales that reveal how social snobbery, class warfare, homosexuality, or a dislike for driving on the left side of the road caused British agents to turn upon each other, patriotism being the least of motivators. All of this is true enough, and perhaps we all need to come back to the raft. Certainly a seriatim reading of spy fiction will tell us much about changing values, about what people take pride in, about trust, and about how one might become world-weary even without betrayal, simply through boredom with a life that has become one long extended slogan. Far more so than the traditional mystery story, which still works within the neat, comfortable constraints of the sonnet that it is, spy fiction has taken off into free-form verse.

Still, the distance from *Kim*, published in 1916, to *The Amateur* by Robert Littell, published in 1981, is covered by another straight line, however much the implications of the form and the moral environment in which it is embedded may have changed. Kim was immensely successful in doing nothing at all; he was a watcher who waited. The story is both real and ideal, filled with homely detail, set in real places one may recognize even today, told in a language that genuinely existed, with an ear to nuance and an eye to color. People die in *Kim*, though generally offstage. Sex exists as an implicit source of jealousy or regard, and once, in Kim's confrontation with a prostitute, more explicitly than we are inclined to remember. But for all the language of the real, there hovers over the best spy stories an atmosphere of the ideal, so that the reader may decide for himself what the intent of the artist has been. The classic spy thriller of Kipling or Buchan is much like a game of chess—a comparison so often made as to be trite, the sacrifice of the pawn being part of the language of cliché so deeply rooted in the literature of duplicity—for it turns on repetition of situations that open lines to infinite variables. Certain strategies, certain gambits, are replayed throughout life and throughout the fiction. When Adam Hall first began to write his spy novels, he called them by customarily trite titles; when they were reprinted nearly twenty years later (Adam Hall and Elleston Trevor now famous names in spy fiction, having created Quiller), these early books were given a different set of conventional titles: *Knight Sinister, Queen in Danger, Bishop in Check, Rook's Gambit, Pawn in Jeopardy.*

The modern spy thriller is not chess, coldly rational, with values attached to each participant, for we do not know the values; backgammon is the game. Vladimir Nabokov could not have written *The Defense* about backgammon, for the essence of the game is attack. One throws the dice; the result is neutral. The testing is in the way one plays the roll. Nothing is either good or bad, and only the playing makes it so. Backgammon, with its magnificent cynicism, is the new conventional wisdom behind the new conventional spies.

Littell has written six books, at least as Littell. The first, *The Defection of A. J. Lewinter,* was a superior cold-war thriller; it won a prize and it glowed with a hard, gemlike intensity. *The Debriefing* came as close to bringing the watcher in from the shadows as one is likely to get. Cold, clear, uncertain, *The Amateur* takes up where Richard Hannay left off, in the modern world. (It also weaves its way back to *Lewinter,* consciously repeating one anecdote and a major plot device.) The amateur is Charlie Heller, who works for the CIA encoding and decoding messages, a technocrat's psychologist, historian, and literary critic working with new languages so far beyond FORTRAN or PASCAL as to have driven Mathematics back to Mystery. He has computer time that he spends on his hobby, searching out in the words of Shakespeare the cryptogram that will, he is certain, produce the name of their real author: Bacon, de Vere, X? He knows his territory as Hannay knew the bush and veldt; he can catch entire meanings between his lips before they are fully off the machine; he knows just where to press, on this letter, right *here*, to turn an entire message into the reasonable nonsense that passes for plausibility at the Company. But he is an amateur in the field; his environment is the unreal world of a cipher room entered with a cipher lock activated to "elbow" (as in "enough elbow room" or "elbow aside and make room"). Outside and beyond his elbow, he is an amateur.

Littell then puts the pieces into place. Heller's girl friend is killed in a terrorist attack on the American consulate in Germany; apparently she has been singled out at random to make the terrorists' point. Heller demands that the CIA, the experts, hunt the terrorists down. The Director refuses. Drawing information from his computer, Heller blackmails the agency into training him so that he may go into the field to kill the terrorists himself. The agency trains him, though badly, and wanting him to fail, sets a trap for him. Once into Czechoslovakia, in pursuit of his targets, Heller finds the local secret police aware of his existence, the CIA determined to eliminate him, and the three terrorists separated, hidden, and progressively alert. Time is running out, as the CIA seeks to retrieve the computer information by which Heller has compelled its cooperation. The landscape unfolds: Prague, the spa at Karlovy Vary, somewhere near Hartford, Connecticut. Heller, the amateur, knows what he knows very well: he is the hedgehog, the CIA the fox in Marx's famous conundrum. He knows all the shorthand systems: Gabelsberger, Schrey, Stolze-Schrey, Marti, Brockaway, Duployé, Sloan-Duployan, Orillana. He has a degree from Yale, where he dissected language, "phonetically, phonemically, grammatically, logically, semantically, historically, statistically and comparatively." He is as at home in this world as were John Buchan's figures in theirs. When with studied arrogance his heroes revealed the empire of their mind by casual references to taking the second turning on the right as one goes up the Khyber Pass, Heller has found the way through his own catch-22. The elemental values have remained constant: justice, revenge (to some the same), pursuit, fear, love, protection.

Buchan and Littell, and certainly Kipling, well illustrate the other bootlegged dividend of spy fiction. Since our spies come not singly but as battalions, we see the landscapes through many eyes, vicariously traveling the world. Verisimilitude requires research, and the best writers do as Gibbon did: they travel over the scenes they are to describe. No writer I have ever read better prepared me for the land around the ancient province of Galloway than John Buchan. Read at, perhaps, eleven, the chase sequence in *The Thirty-Nine Steps* told me exactly the smells and sounds and color of the sky in Scotland, and when finally I climbed Cairnsmore of Fleet, rising to the northeast of Creetown, and the next day walked the lonely country road to Upper Rusko, the road over which the chase sequence passes, it was precisely as Buchan had promised it would be.

Perhaps it is a want of imagination in me, but I could not finish *Tess of the d'Urbervilles* until I spent a rainy night in a side-street hotel in Winchester, Hardy's cathedral city of Wintoncester. D. H. Lawrence's *Kangaroo* was, to my taste, turgid and nasty until the day I sat on the beach at Thirwell, south of Sydney, where he wrote, and read it. Edith Wharton goes down better after a visit to the Mount. Once, for three straight days as another rain on the other side of the world fell, I sat in the Raffles Hotel in Singapore, happily unrenovated, punkah overhead, and read all of the tales of W. Somerset Maugham (and, incongruously, *Up at the Villa*, which reads like James M. Cain, as well). Just as English country-house detective fiction, complete with map of the estate and an *X* where the body was found in the library, helps give us a sense of a once real, now mythical social world of minutiae, so may one travel the world with the thriller, held like the camera up to reality, a reminder of what we have seen, a harbinger of what we will see, and if we are not careful, a substitute for that which we are seeing. Walker Percy's *Moviegoer*, Daniel Boorstin's *Image*, and my homily here contain the same warning: the substitute for reality can become the reality.

Has it not ever been so? Do we not comprehend rage better for *Lear*? Love better for *Pygmalion* (yes, *Pygmalion*)? Death better, in Venice? Lust better for *Hamlet*? Passion better for chess? God better for *Paradise Lost*? Thriller fiction does not, perhaps, keep this company, though it may strive to, and for many who will not contend at the cliff's edge with Lear, it may be the only substitute. There are sausage makers aplenty among the thriller writers, who care not about their research, their logic, their sense of place. In the Victorian age to call something "a sausage" meant that it was somewhat low, perhaps unsavory, as in "sausages and saveloys"; the sausage machines among us that churn out the blockbusters care only for income, and to falsely entertain. Can there be a sillier book in the genre than Robert Ludlum's *Matlock Paper*? Could any author be lazier than the Alistair MacLean who hacked out *Breakheart Pass*, not slowing his typewriter even to reach onto a shelf to verify that the Union Pacific Railroad existed where and when he wished it to? But the genre ought not to be judged by its sausages, any more than one judges a butcher shop by the sawdust on the floor, the book by its cover, or the wine by its cork. One does not measure Charles Dickens by his worst work (nor by his best alone). One does not condemn Edwardian literature because of Frank Harris. One does not assume that all American food comes from Howard Johnson's. There is much quality out there, among the travelers, and good companionship, and one need not assume that Mac-Lean, Ludlum, Pablum & Formula are the only travel agents.

As to travel: a long, looping aside, notwithstanding that my point has been made. (On an excursion, side trips are permissible.) The question is, why are some locales apparently so appropriate to the romantic fiction of spydom, itself the present generation's substitute for the romantic literature of empire, while other locales no less capable of menace and no less colorfully gritty on the screen are ignored? For every thriller set in Minneapolis (Thomas Gifford) there are fifty set in San Francisco. For every detective who operates out of Denver (Rex Burns) there are one hundred in L.A. For every sleuth who worries about truth in Indianapolis (Michael Lewin) there have been a thousand who found and lost it in New York. Canada apparently is an unattractive land for the thriller, though Donald Hamilton put one on the Trans-Canada Highway; and Margaret Millar, in *The Soft Talkers*, in the lake country up north of Toronto, does nicely with territory I know and can attest to. Donald Zochert, who confuses fine writing with good writing, has at last brought Missoula, Montana, onto the map with *Another Crying Woman*, though A. B. Guthrie had done pretty well already with Montana small towns. Philadelphia gets its share, but only K. C. Constantine appears to have discovered the venality in coal-town Pennsylvania, or in a small college town in *The Blank Page*. Obviously the novel of urban violence will dominate, whether in detective or in spy fiction, for that's where the action is said to be, and the parts are more or less interchangeable. One needn't really go to Rome or Moscow; a good set of maps and a guidebook or two, and one can have the hero spinning around the Coliseum and striking out for Gorky Park and the Appian Way.

Having admitted to the falsity of the scene as often set, I must insist that some of the best travel writing done today occurs in the midst of spy and detective fiction. To speak of places I know at first hand: There is more of Tanganyika, in 1954 when still a colony, in David Creed's *Trial of Lobo Icheka* than in any guidebook. There is a more subtle look at relations between the races in South Africa in the books of James McClure (and especially in *The Gooseberry Fool*) than in many a learned piece on apartheid. Small-city, northern Holland (Groningen?) is perfectly captured in *Double-Barrel*, by Nicolas Freeling. Spain as seen by a non-Spaniard is all there, proud and menacing, in Francis Clifford's *Third Side of the Coin*. Armidale, New South Wales, and a thinly disguised University of New England, are analyzed more closely than any sociologist could hope to do in Robert Barnard's *Death of an Old Goat*. And though I have not been to Tibet, I have been up and over that part of the Himalayas by which one drops down from Darjeeling into Gangtok, in Sikkim, and Lionel Davidson's *Rose of Tibet* seemed right there. (While spy fiction best meets the demands of travel literature, the traditional mystery story meets them as well. Else why would so many readers make the pilgrimage, as I have done, to the Reichenbach Falls in Switzerland, or travel to Delfzijl, in the Netherlands, which I have also done, simply to view a statue to the fictional Maigret, on the ground that the first Maigret story, *The Strange Case of Peter the Lett*, occurs there in 1929?) I do not know Florida, but I am convinced that John D. MacDonald has it just right and that Charles Williams had it even better at one time. And though I have been through Alabama, I do not comprehend it, at least not yet, and so I am convinced that Richard North Patterson, in *The Outside Man*, has brought me inside.

Who today, then, has built up the most consistent record

of combining all the elements essential to the formula as given to us by John Buchan, and protected and improved upon that formula, while taking just the proper notice of the necessary tinge of dread, of standing at the dangerous edge? In John Buchan's last, most nearly autobiographical, novel, *Sick Heart River* (in the United States retitled *Mountain Meadow*),* Edward Leithen, a figure who has been the voice of Buchan running through the Hannay series, speaks of this central element in fiction that seeks to illustrate the limits of man's physical, yet equally often moral, endurance: " 'Still I don't understand,' said Leithen. 'He's frightened of the wilds and yet he hankers to get deeper into them, right to a place where nobody's ever been.' "

* This question of title changes is worth close pursuit, though there is no space here. Presumably Houghton Mifflin, Buchan's American publishers, preferred to suggest that *Mountain Meadow* was about a wilderness adventure, as on the surface it is, while the English wanted to acknowledge, as Buchan wished, that the place for which Leithen searched was a metaphor for his own sick heart. One can understand easily enough why Agatha Christie's *Ten Little Niggers* became, in the United States, *Ten Little Indians*, and then, with all ethnicity removed from the title, *And Then There Were None*. It is a little more puzzling that *Murder on the Orient Express*, which evokes one of the world's most romantic journeys, was changed for American readers into *Murder in the Calais Coach*, a title most likely mispronounced, especially in Maine. Apparently Calais coaches are fancier. (In any event, with the motion picture the original title was restored.) Many readers have bought what they thought to be a new Christie to find that it was simply a collection of short stories retitled. This may be good commerce, and publishers are not required to have sympathy for librarians, bibliographers, or scholars, but it may also be simple deceit and greed. Of course, if a motion picture changes the original title for reasons inherent in the visual medium, reprints of the book are likely to bear the new title. Still, can one explain, without hiding behind a spurious argument concerning copyright, why a 1981 paperback reprint of Nicolas Freeling's *Over the High Side* (1971) should be entitled *The Lovely Ladies* and why not one word appears, on jacket, in text, or even on copyright page, to say that it is the same book?

Who are the natural heirs, then, to Eric Ambler, the early Graham Greene, to Buchan, the best in their trade-craft? There are many: Noel Behn in *The Kremlin Letter*, Lionel Davidson in *The Night of Wenceslas*, Ted Allbeury in *Moscow Quadrille*, Francis Clifford in *The Naked Runner*, the early Manning Coles of *Drink to Yesterday* and *A Toast to Tomorrow* (after which they went off dread-fully), Martin Woodhouse in *Tree Frog*, and of course John le Carré. But le Carré is by now, like the later Greene, a bit preoccupied with profundities, so that while he is undoubtedly the best of a class group, he is not truly in the tradition, content to let the tale carry its own convictions. "Better fewer but better," Lenin's final admonition, applies to many of those writers who, taken up with "the fourth man" theme, sometimes forget that the structure of the genre requires a sense of movement.

Rather, I would choose nine other writers, six British and three American, as more truly representative of the trends in the traditional spy thriller as spoken in demotic English. Unlike Thomas Hardy, who clearly influenced le Carré (as he noted in a recent interview), these writers do not feel that they must address larger injustices through the petty, individualized (or even institutional) ones they describe; they are content to do that which Kipling did: spin a yarn, letting irony carry such other levels of meaning as a reader may wish to attribute to the yarn out of his own experience. All but one of these nine has a clear track record: each has written more than a dozen thrillers and lives by doing so (the exception in my list is William F. Buckley, Jr., who lives to write though he needn't). Each is worth a moment.

Three of these writers may be grouped together: Berkeley Mather, Gavin Lyall, and Desmond Bagley. Mather is the closest to Kipling, for India and the high snow ranges of the Northwest Frontier are his territory. He served in the

British army in India, worked with the intelligence corps, and has settled into retirement, name changed from J.E.W. Davies, near Rye, in Sussex. He has spun out twelve novels to which he admits and at least one that is omitted from his customary bibliography. Not all are equally good, but those that concentrate on the Buchan formula and the Kipling themes have no match: *The Pass Beyond Kashmir, The Break in the Line, The White Dacoit*. One tastes the yak butter, smells the Sherpas, sidles up to the barrack rats, and chokes on the inadequate "dust distance" intervals between vehicles in convoy, exploring in the end the whole of India from the Pakistani to the Burmese borders, with lengthy stops on the Malabar Coast in between. John Masters can do it no better.

Gavin Lyall is concerned with men who are on the shadow line, operating just inside the law, yet strongly moral where justice and personal ethics are concerned. He writes brilliantly descriptive set pieces, though his plotting remains loose. He knows airplanes, cars, cameras, and guns, and he brings a sense of relevant expertise to his use of technology to further the plot. Perhaps the most nearly perfect clone of a Buchan novel is Lyall's *Midnight Plus One,* where movement across relatively little-known European landscapes, ambivalence of purpose, and a crack-of-doom deadline are combined most effectively. *The Most Dangerous Game*, in which the hero is stalked, occupies the same space taken up so nicely by Geoffrey Household in *Rogue Male* or *A Rough Shoot. The Wrong Side of the Sky* is about old friends who must decide between their friendship and their integrity. These are well-worn themes, and Lyall's talents are those of a skilled journalist who reworks familiar territory to conclusions that appear fresh. More recently Lyall has become too ambitious, and his latest book, *The Secret Servant*, encroaches ineffectively into le Carré, Len Deighton, and Joseph Hone (whose *Oxford Gambit* does it so much better) territory, where the boffins and bureaucrats have at each other over soggy definitions of the national good. At his best, however, Lyall captures that sense of Judas country (the title of one of his books) in which all espionage fiction takes place.

Of the three, Desmond Bagley has come the farthest fastest. He began as an imitation Alistair MacLean or Hammond Innes, but as these writers became lost in almost mechanistic churning and sloppy research (MacLean) or overblown dialogue and tedious description (Innes), Bagley grew. The early books of the mid-1960s, *The Golden Keel* and *High Citadel*, were virtually interchangeable with MacLean and Innes of the same period. By *Running Blind* (1970), which brilliantly uses a landscape to which I can attest, Iceland, and in *The Freedom Trap* (1972), which ups the ante to ask the kinds of moral questions the young Ambler had asked (and about which he too was becoming tedious by the '70s), Bagley had found a voice of his own, a voice in a chorus to be sure, as trained by Buchan and company, but with a distinctive sound nonetheless. After an unhappy diversion into New Zealand, where Bagley seems not to have listened carefully (*The Snow Tiger*), he has returned to familiar territory, and in *The Enemy* provides the answer already well stated by the immortal Pogo. By *Flyaway* Bagley was back in the Buchan camp with what may properly qualify for the dust-jacket cliché, a "breakneck chase thriller" with all the stigmata showing. Bagley makes the landscape do much of his work, and except for the South Island of New Zealand, he endows terrain with the attributes of a character with a will of its own. Attention to detail (*Flyaway* contains three tiny errors that a historian of Francophone North Africa might catch), careful research without excess, and good judgment about the impact of violence on his readers, place Bagley at the very top of the British thriller writers, a group that is superior to the Americans at their best.

This is not to be dismissive of the Americans, for they are working out of a somewhat different tradition. They know their Buchan, and at first glance the formula may be the same, but they also know Cooper's Leatherstocking Tales, and the function of Western fiction in American popular culture. Men work more nearly alone, and with a greater intensity of concentration on the menacing aspects of the terrain, than in British fiction. They are more violent, and they anticipate violence more quickly. They are almost never worried about matters of class, as Bagley's or Mac-Lean's heroes appear to be. And the Americans are more inclined to credit conspiracy, even from one's best friends, than the British writers, Greene and le Carré notwithstanding. Because treachery is anticipated, it is taken into account by the hero in defining the relationship originally, so that if he does not, of necessity, kill the treasonous friend, he may well remain a friend, the two simply amoral men who wound up fighting on different sides in a civil war.

The best at this kind of writing is Ross Thomas, who also writes as Oliver Bleeck, so unlikely a name that one suspects it, and not Thomas, is the real one, despite the information (some of it patently misleading) that Thomas gives out to those who ask him about himself. There are at least nineteen books and not one of them is bad. From the beginning, with *The Cold War Swap* (1966), Thomas created real people who spoke real sentences of the kind one might expect to hear while sitting around a bar in Chicago, Washington, or L.A. Probably no one writes truer dialogue, though Chandler and Stout wrote more amusing lines. The relationship between men is tough, unsentimental, honest; women have their own toughness, though it is different. People use each other, and understand that this is part of the social contract. And locales are not only integral to the action, they influence the speech rhythms: conversations in Washington always carry a hint of the political, and good talk in Albertia, an ill-disguised Nigeria, is not interchangeable with throwaway lines among the Libyans, to contrast *The Seersucker Whipsaw* (1967) with *The Mordida Man* (1981). Good as they were, the earlier books pandered a little; but sudden, gratuitous sexual scenes used, apparently, to reveal character (Thomas had a thing about fellatio), and speech patterns of nonwhite participants that came out of an open Aunt Jemima box, have nearly disappeared. The books remain bawdy, bloody, complex, minutely crafted, and very American: laid-back and likable.

Another very American writer in the tradition of the Great Game is Donald Hamilton, who has created a series figure, Matt Helm, who is a killing machine, as distant from Thomas's unheroic heroes as one can find. Helm's humor is all inward, sardonic, self-destructive. He trusts only himself and he has absolutely no friends, even inside the agency for which he works. He goes where he is told and does what he must. Beneath the hard shell is a man wishing he could find someone to believe in, knowing that governments, indeed all institutions by their very nature, use people until they are used up, and fearing that he may use up anyone he gets too close to. Helm, retired from his agency job, returns to it when his marriage falls apart. He knows guns, cars, compasses, and how to smell danger on the wind. Some have compared him to Travis McGee, though Matt Helm is a bit closer to Mickey Spillane, for he treats women as true equals, which means that he will shoot one in the back if he must, without that moment of hesitation (and paragraph of philosophy) that slows McGee's reaction time. Ross Thomas gives us mature women, as well-read and as informed about sex as the men. Most reviewers of his *Eighth Dwarf* noted with appropriate delight how a young woman, at first apparently the object of a Thomas parody, spoke only in the style of the Victorian literature with which she spent her professional life; when she beds the hero, he finds that she has read everything in the British Museum's famed locked cabinet of Victorian pornography as well. Helm would merely be disgusted, for he likes his sex to come dressed in buttons and bows, as he remembers it in childhood. Hamilton, Helm's creator, may be poking just a wee bit of fun at the American image, Swedish born as he is, but for the most part he ambushes, ravages, shadows, devastates, betrays, menaces, poisons, intrigues, intimidates, retaliates, terrorizes, silences, removes, and terminates (to cite the one-word titles he has applied to most of the Matt Helm series) with the skill of a Mike Hammer, the speed of a James Bond, and the anger at a ravaged America of a Travis McGee. From *Death of a Citizen* in 1960 (preceded by *Assignment: Murder*, in 1956, behind which title deserving of any teacher's rip-apart muscle power lurks a finely attuned encounter with death among piñon scrub and pine in New Mexico) to a possibly unwise experiment with substantially weightier fiction in *The Mona Intercept* in 1980, Hamilton has not only been (as so often described) "the American James Bond," he has been better than Ian Fleming book for book.*

* I have written elsewhere on Donald Hamilton; see "The Sordid Truth," *New Republic*, July 26, 1975. In the intervening years Hamilton has continued to seem to me the best of that large body of authors who write "original paperbacks," but I won't rehearse the reasons here, since I have argued them all before, especially in

The third American completes a triangle, for he is equally distant from Thomas and Hamilton: William F. Buckley, Jr. One might argue that his track record is not yet clear, there being only three spy thrillers from him, but surely his column has long revealed how he feels about the range of subjects McGee, Helm, or Thomas's McCorkle and Padillo, early series figures, dilate upon: women's lib, the declining quality of a good martini, fast food, the welfare junkie, tinsmiths' cars, condominium rip-offs, road hogs, and confused liberals. Buckley belongs in our group because he writes and plots extremely well, because he has a sense of humor that is so calibrated in its mid-Atlantic position as to be the very intonation of the English-Speaking Union as ought to be, and because he has taken the formula, and, while poking fun at all its excrescences, had hewed to its central line with a beguiling ambiguity. Reading Buckley is rather like playing backgammon and chess simultaneously and losing at both while enjoying it. His beloved ambivalence leads him to sign off in letters, "Bend, as ever."

The first Buckley book, *Saving the Queen*, is full of inside knowledge of how the archives at Windsor Castle work, and how a registrar at Yale might recruit a young student in Davenport College into the CIA, and how to fly an airplane. Since the hero, Blackford Oakes, is at home in all Anglo-American upper-class circumstances, he makes a major sacrifice for his country and takes the Queen of England to bed. Richard Hannay would not have approved, but it's a new way to fight the continuing American Revolution. Beneath this drawing-room comedy, stylishly written and

---

relation to the use of the "series figure," and readers are not fond of authors who pad out their manuscripts with warmed-over phrases from earlier publications. Neither should any writer be, which is one reason Spillane is not discussed in this essay.

impeccably handcrafted, is a clear political message: ends do sometimes justify means. This seems just fine to me, since I have never grasped why certain moralists consider an argument concluded by charging an opponent with having used the ends to justify the means; death comes as the end, as Agatha Christie tells us, and ought we not rail against the darkness of the light? Of course the ends justify the means; otherwise there would be neither spy fiction nor survival.

Next came *Stained Glass*, set in the Germany of the 1950s, when the United States still had some choices to make. Count Axel Wintergrin is shaking the canebrakes all the way to Louisiana by running a political campaign, which he might well win, based on a demand for a unified fatherland. The CIA thinks this not a good idea, though Wintergrin is no Communist, and in the end Oakes plays an acutely ambivalent role in dispatching Wintergrin from the scene. The title reminds us of the medieval complexity of politics, American as well as European, and, moreover, of the fragility, and need for care that goes into the creation, of a great monument, whether a cathedral, a political philosophy, or an alliance. The political argument is almost jesuitical, certainly baroque, and some would find it perverse. Muted literary allusions drop like faded cherry blossoms on every page. Allen Dulles, Dean Acheson, and other people less real than Blackford Oakes move in and out, reminding the reader that, with a bit more courage, the United States might have cast Europe in a different mold. (The question of whether the United States ought to have done so is left unasked, though not unsuggested.) The death of Wintergrin was probably not "necessary" in any philosophically valid sense of the word; in the end Oakes and Dulles agree. They agree, too, that a failure to act because, in acting, one may be conclusively proved wrong is no way to behave in a tough world. To prevent Stalin's invasion of the West—about which he almost certainly was bluffing—Oakes has been required to eliminate one of the West's next best hopes. In being Judas, Oakes prevents a possibility and destroys a longer-range probability. Not baroque but Byzantine, these political views; and in the world of the new Byzantium, Buckley is closer to the bone than le Carré. *Who's on First?*, the third novel, elevates this ethical dilemma out into space, to the world of astronauts and satellites, Russia and the United States engaged in one long sequence out of Abbott and Costello. The question is, however, not who is on first, but who is the straight man?

These authors, British and American, give us the form, the structure, and the ideology of spy fiction. They show us why such fiction is both part of, and apart from, detective and mystery fiction. Purists draw clear distinctions between these bodies of thought: a mystery need not involve a detective; a thriller may encompass amateurs while spy fiction is more delimiting; detective fiction is (or is not, according to the writer, usually spinning an article out of a master's thesis) the same as procedural police fiction. Gothic romances, horror stories, the pure puzzles of Poe and the raddled puzzles of Carr, belong more to the old tradition of riddle stories. All these distinctions are interesting to entertain on a snowy evening, though there is more to be found in common in the continuum from spy through detective to mystery to riddle to gothic story than in the differentiations. All these authors create a world for us that at first we recognize and then, with growing awareness, we know is not our world.

Of course, plot and attitude are not the only ways by which the genre may be broken into categories to make the splitters happy, nor are they the sole element at work in defining a subspecies. The question of style remains central to all fiction, and Len Deighton and Adam Hall between them have contributed in particular to a new style. Deighton began with exceptionally elliptical prose, as though the synapses of logic were malfunctioning. *Horse Under Water* (dope, drowned), which appeared in 1962, misleads the reader not only by plot and words but by sentence structure and paragraphing. At about the same time Elleston Trevor, writing as Adam Hall, employed the same stylistic devices, constructing paragraphs that read as though every other sentence had been left out, compiling evidence backwards so that the reader was left running in sand. Some readers were inordinately annoyed by Deighton and Hall, though they were doing nothing more intrinsically irritating than applying the stylistic devices of several then-fashionable French writers to a genre in which fashion was more than ordinarily conservative.

As they developed, Deighton and Hall moved in different directions, though they remained the primary innovators with respect to the form of the spy story. Deighton eventually arrived at the thriller based on counterfactual history, a technique dear to the hearts of some historians who believe that, by deleting a single fact from reality and then arguing all other "true facts" to a conclusion, they can best judge what the primary cause of an event was. In history, a counterfactual question might read, "If we posit that slavery did not exist in the Southern states in any form in the 1850s, would there have been a Civil War?" By asking such a question, the historian hopes to place relative weights upon the other causes to which the Civil War is ascribed: the Northern tariff, incompatible cultures, land hunger. Most of the sources of conflict were capable of compromise; slavery was not. *Ergo*, slavery was the primary cause of the Civil War. Deighton has taken the same approach with World War II and the cold war. In *SS-GB* (1979) he begins with the assumption that Britain has been occupied by Nazi Germany, Churchill executed, and the royal family has escaped to exile. From this premise he shapes a combination of detective story and spy thriller that runs a resistance movement and an ordinary investigation by an inspector from Scotland Yard, doing his job as he must even in an occupied country, on a collision course. The result is a challenge to many of our assumptions about duty, justice, and, most obviously, how history determines who will wear the white and who the black hats. In 1981 Deighton extended this technique (badly) in *XPD*, which presupposes that Churchill and Hitler met in secret, the British prime minister asking Hitler to leave Britain free in exchange for having his way with the Jews and the surrender to him of the British Empire, to the point that the British government unsuccessfully and briefly sought to suppress Deighton's work. Thus did style, blent with an unacceptable counterfactual proposition, dramatize the public value of such fiction.

Adam Hall, on the other hand, drove his stylish vehicle in the opposite direction. Quiller, introduced and fleshed out in *The Quiller Memorandum* (1965), *The Ninth Directive* (1966), and *The Striker Portfolio* (1969), is a thinking machine. In these early books he knows to the second how long it will take for a drug to fog his brain. By the 1970s Quiller has become the machine, every movement mechanically dictated by scientific knowledge of body chemistry, of friction and physics, or of the speed of sound. Since Quiller works for "the Bureau," a shadow executive so secret even the British government does not know of its activities, and since he must accept his assignments as mathematical givens (though he has his own way of rebelling), his every move seems Pavlovian, conditioned by institution, instruction, and artificial intelligence. Quiller doesn't permit what he calls gut-think:

> Check map. Check time. The landmark was thirty miles from the frontier and the clock gave me three minutes to go. I waited thirty seconds and eased the control column back a degree and held it and flattened out again at four hundred feet and looked for the hills and saw their shadows this side of them in the lower half of the windscreen. They were sliding towards me in a soft green wave and I wanted to climb again to increase the margin of safety but that was gut-think because the briefing sources were first-class and these hills were down at three hundred feet and the margin was as much as I could afford without starting to show up on someone's radar screen. Two minutes. [*The Sinkiang Executive*]

Thus is Quiller hurled over Soviet airspace in Slingshot, an SX-454, below radar pickup, making for the People's Republic of China. He does not bother to provide an antecedent to "their" and "they" for he was already programmed to expect an attempt at interception at about this point. The index finger to his left hand is missing: "I caught it between two planks at the edge of the dockside as I went over." We learn no more (this loss of a spare part occurs in *The Kobra Manifesto*) about pain or pride or how two years later he could survive his fight with his Russian clone:

> He moved very fast and pain flared in my arm as the pressure came on—he was going to break it and I curved a thumb-shot for the eye and missed and struck again and missed and went on striking until his head rolled back and I felt the softness of the eye but he

was strong in his rage and heaved himself up again with an animal sound, his big hands reaching to hold me while his boot crashed down on the snow beside my head, going to be no go because he wasn't human, he was a crazed mind empowering muscle and motor nerves with the force of a monster and its intention was to kill and it would do it because it was programmed to do it. . . . *Don't think. Move.*

Quiller has no identity except when under the pressure of his work. He is a watcher, though not without, at the center of the action, detached, clinically observing his own death throes, aware to a millimeter how much more movement he can get out of his body when oiled with sweat than he can when it is dry. He refers to himself as "the organism," and while he knows that brain-think is vital to preparation, he blocks out all but his automatic responses when, like the animal he still is, his sense of mortal danger is aroused. Disembodied, utterly rational, Quiller may well prove another two novels or so along the line to actually have been a machine all the time, constructed from a mating of a nerve-gas canister and an automatic timing device. Hall has turned his style to the service of this machine. Perhaps he has had to, for he has written at least eighty-five books (he was born in 1920), several plays, and seen his share of work turned into motion pictures. Though English, he lives in Arizona, and more than any other writer he represents the ultimate evolution of the Buchan formula, the complete application of Conan Doyle's scientific method to the human body, the final stage short of science fiction in creating the nerveless operative who, if he must, will destroy himself to achieve his goal. No writer is so claustrophobic for his readers, none so distant, and few so skilled in the technique of totally neutralizing all moral issues when they meet on the killing ground. Of all his books, *The Tango Briefing* (1973) will stand as a classic of its kind, for in it the machine thinks its way through to a kind of salvation based upon the knowledge of so simple a matter as pressure and pain:

> In the confused cerebral state there was only one area with any kind of ability to reason, and here the technician in me was observing the situation in his own terms and noting things like the complementary factors of requirements and facilities available, the requirements being to press the activator and detonate the device [a nuclear device, to be detonated with Quiller on top of it], the facilities being my thumb and its motor nerves.

And so he finds some other motor nerves, to a cackling, grisly conclusion.

Yet in the end one returns to a writer who has not moved the formula forward but simply employed it with consummate skill. No trend setter, though my personal favorite, William Haggard continues each year to give us one more episode in the curiously civilized life of Colonel Charles Russell of Security Executive. Haggard is a professional's professional. He uses no tricks to reach the shadow line between appearances and reality, being a master of upper-class (some would say snobbish) British nuance. One has to know how to read English English well to take his meaning. Russell is the kind of man who cannot remain retired. He had "a pension and a little money, hobbies like golf and some elegant fishing, the good health to enjoy a still vigorous life. Above all he had friends and not all were eminent. Some of them weren't even English." English reviewers have found Haggard (who, "in real life," is

Richard Clayton, an intelligence officer in the Indian army during the Second World War) suffocatingly class-conscious, given to in-jokes and nauseating social know-how. American readers, perhaps because they do not recognize all the asides about port wine, the alleged racial innuendo, or the real meaning of remarks about "limousine liberals," and also because they are less concerned about those class connotations they do recognize, have greeted Haggard more warmly. There is a bit of Anthony Powell, and something of Dickens, and of Jane Austen, and quite a lot of Mrs. Gaskell in Haggard, and there is that fine English love for language and especially for puns.

Haggard's titles, like his plots, are more intricate than they seem. Some contain those puns. *Venetian Blind* contains two. *The Telemann Touch* is about a paid assassin with an uncommon touch with people; *The Arena* is about the financial City of London caught up in a duel; *The Unquiet Sleep* is about drug usage and an unsleeping government; *Yesterday's Enemy* is, perhaps, about Germany. Behind these titles Haggard takes people as they come: terrorist Japanese, slyly neutral Swiss, French leaders who still hate the British, Americans who do not much like the English, tinpot dictators from Latin America who can be taught to follow the "higher self-interest," "some ape in Africa [Amin]," a thoroughly sensible and resourceful third generation West Indian. *The Bitter Harvest* is a typically complex story in which Colonel Russell watches rather than acts. A back-bencher in the House of Commons, Maurice Pater, whose integrity will not permit compromising his way to the front ranks, is enticed into supporting a cause the public believes doubtful: apartheid. He sees that he is being used, backs away, and so must be assassinated. But look more closely: the assassin is a black African; integrity may rest in the defense of apartheid.

The world's morality and an individual's integrity are thrown into conflict—not unusual, this—in a form the reverse of that which virtually all readers of thriller fiction have come to take for granted. Haggard does not side with the South Africans: he merely observes.

Still, Russell is not ambivalent. He knows who he is and what he believes, and he feels no need to apologize. In *The Scorpion's Tail* a band of American, British, and Swedish hippies, high on pot and LSD, briefly seize control of an island off Málaga. The Spanish owner and Russell are agreed upon waiting:

> ". . . And on my island they're having a last blind orgy."
>
> "Singing I imagine."
>
> "Yes. May I ask how you knew?"
>
> "They always sing when they're certain they've had it. It's a song called 'We Shall Not Be Moved.' When they've sung it twice they always are."
>
> "You're not sympathetic, then?"
>
> "Of course not. But nor am I exactly hostile. I'm sorry for unfortunate children."
>
> "All very liberal. All very British."
>
> "Naturally. Since that's what I am."

In every instinct, Haggard is entirely conservative. Rather like Buchan. But also ready to do battle. In *The Power House* he unflatteringly depicted a prime minister then in office. *The Poison People* was sharply attacked, perhaps because of how it handled an easily identifiable leftist. Another book was the subject of a formal diplomatic protest, and subsequently Haggard was not allowed to mention Malta, Libya, or Egypt in *The Median Line*, though all are immediately recognizable under their

[78]

masquerades, Malta being "the Island." *The Bitter Harvest* fared badly in the United States because of its alleged racism. Sex is never explicit, though necessarily present, and the language is always elegant, but many readers find Haggard unconventional, brutal, entirely too realistic in his cool, well-bred prose. Perhaps Haggard *is* setting a trend after all: as Eric Ambler is said to have turned spy fiction to the left, Haggard may be a British Buckley. In the tradition of the spymasters, his cerebral figures still believe in a sense of order.

Spy fiction asks, What's going on? It attempts to account for events already transpired and to control events yet to come. Most often evidence must be read backwards, inferred from events. To this extent spy fiction is at the far end of the continuum from traditional mystery fiction, which begins by setting the scene, introducing the characters, usually killing one of them, and then reconstructing what must have happened. There really is no doctrine of fair play in spy fiction, for it operates from different assumptions. It is clearly at the growing end of the continuum, drawing plots from the headlines. That it is growing and that the classic locked-room puzzle-mystery is in recession is hardly surprising, though it is further evidence of how the genre reflects and follows society. It is our particular ministry of fear.

6

T HE DETECTIVE STORY permits us to move
up close to sins that we could not, for ourselves,
contemplate. Perhaps this is why the detective story so
often is said to be therapeutic: it provides the nightmares
of morality that we cannot otherwise meet directly. While
spy fiction is, at base, all action—even when mixed with
deceit, landscape, and intelligent dialogue, movement is
the key to the thriller—the mystery novel, though a puzzle,
is primarily an investigation of character in relation to
crime as society defines it. While the fears we entertain are
worn water-smooth in our dreams, the written word brings
those fears to the surface, externalizes them, and best of all,
in the end gives them a plausible, even rational, explanation. Perhaps one reason John Dickson Carr and Carter
Dickson, one and the same, are intolerable upon rereading
is that they are utterly abstracted from any reality one
might imagine: the reality of the street, of the boudoir, of
the police cell, of the nightmare. They produced puzzles
written at length, wherein character is not only allowed
scant play, character is virtually never the explanation of
the mystery itself. Yet, in any genuine mystery, of fiction
or of fact, the answer arises from character.

The difference between detective fiction and (for example) Émile Zola's *Thérèse Raquin* is found only in the
mind of the critic. Thérèse's lover murders her husband by
drowning him; by clever manipulation, the lover is able to
wed the widow without suspicion; yet both are haunted by
the specter of the dead spouse. For such a plot Zola is said
to be a naturalist, realistically showing his readers how

human beings respond to stimuli as animals must. A similar plot in the hands of James M. Cain, in *The Postman Always Rings Twice*, is seen less as a contribution to American realism in the manner of Dreiser's *Sister Carrie* and more as a lesser detective story, until Cain is rediscovered by the *Paris Review*. Yet who is to say Cain writes less well than Zola, especially since most American readers will have encountered Zola only in mediocre translation? And what is the gap that separates Zola and Cain, each respected in his own way, from the many murder mysteries constructed to precisely this plot? A sense of style? Surely, rather, a sense of the nightmare, and its closeness to us, that has been successfully exorcised.

The peculiar pleasures of the detective story have been examined by many writers, a good number of them not academics.* There is some agreement on the characteristics shared with much other fiction. The mystery story, and many detective stories (with the frequent exception of the so-called procedural school), is marked with a sense of irony. Again the line from Trollope's *Barchester Towers* through C. P. Snow's *The Masters* (itself a kind of mystery) to Reginald Hill (*A Clubbable Woman* or *A Killing Kindness*, for examples) is direct enough. The exposure of hypocrisy, often social, is a persistent element, and while one would not endow all of Rex Stout's wry observations, placed in the mouth of Nero Wolfe, with the same subtlety one finds in Thackeray's *Vanity Fair*, the appeal often is in the pricking of similar bubbles. The tone and shape of Arnold Bennett's *Riceyman Steps* are, surely, all that one can ask for in a mystery, lacking only the murder.

Of course, comparisons like these infuriate many readers.

---

* The reference here is to Erik Routley's *Puritan Pleasures of the Detective Story* (London, 1972).

On the one hand, some critics attempt to claim for a body of dubious fiction some dignity by virtue of what may, by others, be dismissed as a specious affinity. On the other hand, for those intent upon using detective fiction to define popular culture, which in turn is used to defend one or another ideological position concerning subjects and people allegedly ignored by establishment history and criticism, the breaking down of barriers is seen as harmful, making self-conscious critical analysis of the detective story useless. This is, of course, precisely my point: that the detective story must not be analyzed in a self-consciously separate way, and that it appeals to the same needs within us that much other fiction appeals to.

But it does more than this, or there would be no excursion, no itinerary, no countryside to be explored. Detective fiction does have a route, an agenda, of its own. As already suggested, it is concerned with guilt, deception, and logic, subjects on a continuum and at tension with each other. Because it is especially concerned with deceit, the mystery novel or play ought never to be precisely what it seems. Yet there are practical problems that stand in the way of total deceit, so that most readers anticipate a resolution in the end. What can one do, after all, with the artifact, the book, *this* object held in the hand? In a conventional novel, the number of pages left between event x and the final page of print offers few clues to what may follow. In detective fiction, those pages betray the plot, for a "solution" to the mystery (provided the formal mystery, "who done it," is the principal concern of author or reader) that is offered up thirty pages from the end of the book is known to be a red herring. The reader understands that there are to be new surprises in the pages that remain. Some few writers have been able to overcome this simple physical problem, though never more than once: the false confession at which

Agatha Christie was the master, by which a suspect is cleared, only to be proved later actually to have committed the crime, allows the suspense to continue to the end, but it does not really eliminate the simple fact that at any given point the reader is at x-plus-y pages from the conclusion and will take the distance over which the excursion must yet pass as *the* major clue. Unlike the circumstances of most deaths, the fiction of death reveals in advance just when the end will occur.

The cleverer yet weaker writers, recognizing the nature of the artifact held in the hand, fall prey to the temptation to heap sensation upon sensation in the final pages, following double with triple and Maltese crosses, to the point of losing all touch with the logic that has shaped their discourse before. (There are exceptions, certainly, as in Robert Littell's *Debriefing*, in which the final twist, though expected, is not expected in precisely the form it takes, or in some of the best work of Robert Barnard. Both these writers, incidentally, are or appear to be academics, who have studied the craft before becoming practitioners of it.) The highest praise is, for such writers, to have kept the reader guessing "to the last page." This, being false to life, often makes for poor fiction, though not invariably.

The desire to surprise, indeed the necessity of surprise, is among the so-called limitations of the detective novel. Yet surprise, if not of event then of motivation, is at the core of most literature; even that which proceeds inexorably to an expected conclusion surprises by the way in which it shows how it is that a given conclusion was, in truth, inevitable. The logic of Kafka's *Trial* is, in this sense, like the logic of Sherlock Holmes: a logic not to be denied. It is the logic of the Dostoevski of *The Idiot* rather than of *Crime and Punishment*.

Perhaps this need to surprise, to show that there is no

end to deceit, to life as recovered by fiction, even to the artifact, the book, is best caught by Anthony Shaffer in his play *Sleuth*. To a play, the listing of the characters in the playbill is the artifactual equivalent of the number of pages left in the book or the number of grooves visibly remaining to be heard from the disk: one "knows" that what will have happened will be shaped by the appearance of each person listed in the cast. For *Sleuth*, which is both a genuine mystery and a parody of mysteries, Shaffer provided a list of characters in the playbill who do not exist in the play, so that one cannot anticipate the end. Some reviewers called this "cunning dishonesty" in much the way Ronald Knox and his crowd attacked Christie for Roger Ackroyd; yet what rule of the theater tells us that the list of characters need be honest, or that the playbill too cannot become part of the play? The lesson the critic Walter Kerr read from Shaffer's audacity was that "you can't make a mystery of an open book" and that one ought not to pass out programs; this is precisely the wrong lesson, since time and again mysteries are made of open books.

Shaffer went further, I believe, for to me the final resolution to the double and triple cross of *Sleuth* does not stand revealed in the formal play itself, and is not concealed through the playbill, but rather is made explicit only at the last conceivable moment: by the sequence in which the cast takes the curtain call. By this sequence a different order of death is revealed, and through the curtain call, the meaning of the events displayed before us onstage is reversed. (The problem here is rather like the doctrine of flux mixed with the Heisenberg principle: once one is onto the rôle of the playbill, and once one "knows" that the curtain calls are an integral part of the play, the presence of the observer has changed the play itself, so that it can never work again as it did in first production, or on opening night, or for the individual viewer on first sight. Further, *Sleuth* becomes impossible to translate into a motion picture, since the credits cannot be held in the hand in the form of a playbill, and there are no curtain calls; the screen adaptation is a fine picture with emphasis on character—through superlative acting by Michael Caine and Sir Laurence Olivier—and notwithstanding a "faithful" adherence to the plot of the original play, a resolution that is quite different.) Shaffer has created an underliterature that subverts the theatrical form.

Writers like Shaffer are the bandits of the genre. Just as society defines crime, and criminals then conform to those definitions, readers will attempt to define "the mystery," and will force upon writers the need to transgress. Precisely because the detective story generally has a clear structure to it, a structure derived from the normative arguments concerning empirical reality, there will be those who, in seeking to junk the structure, will provide it with new dimensions. They will do to, and for, detective fiction what William Gibson, for example, did to, and for, autobiography when he wrote *A Mass for the Dead*: the language of convention serves the ends of subversion, making that open book a closed one.

7

B ᴜᴛ ᴡʜᴀᴛ ᴏ ғ the structure of detective fiction as
normally pursued? Even an excursion, permissive as
it is of byways, must include the familiar scenes that lie
along its path. The structure of mystery and detective
fiction as followed by the grand masters of the past flows
logically, and we should examine that flow, since the great
majority of readers gain much of their pleasure from
seeing the structure adhered to flawlessly, the ambiguities
they best tolerate arising from meaning and the manipulation of words, not from the structure itself. As suggested
earlier, they may appreciate the suspense of the huddle
and have empathy with the quarterback, but they want the
game to be played out inside the limits of the normal field
and to the running of the normal clock. The reader of
detective fiction enjoys the divine tension between the
exact and the unknown, and if there are no exact boundaries
that circumscribe the unknown, there can be (for most) no
tension. Order matters, details count, and integrity is served
by excess.

The formula for detective or mystery fiction is far more
complex than the formula for spy or thriller fiction, and to
say that both are formulaic is to say very little. The
simplest of thrillers need fall only into a natural trini-
tarianism: produce the hero, put him up a tree and throw
rocks at him, get him down from the tree. Detective and
mystery fiction involve eight, or perhaps nine, distinct
stages of construction, each stage having subformulaic con-
ventions of its own. Upon each of these stages the writer
will place his own personal touch, and the stages need not

follow with the same logic, the same sense of sequence produced by necessity, as in thriller fiction. For this reason the detective story often is said to be infinitely more complex than the thriller, though dealing with the same issues of guilt, responsibility, and deceitful cause.

One begins by defining the subject. The subject must then be kept from the reader, so that the subject appears to be otherwise. Ross Macdonald is an adept at this, for the subject invariably will appear to be the search for a lost person, often a child, while the "real" subject will be buried unto the fifth generation, and since we expect this, yet another "real" subject will remain yet behind the mirror. Macdonald's plots are therefore predictable at one level; because they are also complex, serious, and Freudian, they are taken to heart by critics who normally ignore the problem of mysteries. Macdonald draws upon Raymond Chandler as Chandler drew from Dashiell Hammett. These writers have modernized Leatherstocking, have brought the legends of chivalric romance to the New World, giving us wandering knights rescuing distressed damsels who prove to be as tarnished as the American Dream. In the United States the detective is, most likely but not always, a private operative, and in two senses of the word: he does not work within an institution, the police, who are conventionally seen as corrupt or at least corruptible, the solution being part of the problem; and he is private, inward, to himself, unwilling to be co-opted by society and a little sentimental about his independence. The private eye is the natural child of the man with the long gun, of Longrifle who led his horse through the eastern forests, of the man who mounted that horse and rode into town as Shane, to save society from itself since, as it grew more civilized and more complicated, it lost the elemental instincts for survival. The Western hero, alone against the sky, ready to do society's killing for it, to ride the gunmen out of town, to protect sheepherders from cattlemen, was also private, inward, and ready to move on to right wrongs to be found elsewhere at the cutting edge of society. The West was won, the frontier closed, virgin land was no more, the rugged individualist was simply a wisecracking subordinate climbing the corporate ladder, and the long ribbon of asphalt had found its way to Malibu. The Western came home to roost in the detective story of Chandler and Macdonald and their many imitators, in the streets of Los Angeles and in the hills above Santa Barbara, where the sins of the Last Chance Saloon seemed innocent in retrospect as one walked the boulevards filled with porn shows, snuff films, and child prostitution. The land had run out, and the cowboy rode in off the plains, climbed down from his mustang and into his Mustang, and took to the thruways of nostalgia, muttering *Farewell, My Lovely* as he drove into the sunset.

The subject, then, is the modern condition. Raymond Chandler's famous essay, "The Simple Art of Murder," defends this bleak, burned-out view as an accurate statement about a real world:

> It is not a fragrant world, but it is the world you live in, and certain writers with tough minds and a cool spirit of detachment can make very interesting and even amusing patterns out of it. It is not funny that a man should be killed, but it is sometimes funny that he should be killed for so little, and that his death should be the coin of what we call civilization. All this still is not quite enough.
>
> In everything that can be called art there is a quality of redemption. It may be pure tragedy, if it is high tragedy, and it may be pity and irony, and it may

[88]

be the raucous laughter of the strong man. But down these mean streets a man must go who is not himself mean, who is neither tarnished nor afraid.

Any addicted reader of detective fiction has heard this last line so often it has taken on the quality of gospel. It is also sentimental and impossible, and Chandler knew that it was both, for you cannot go untarnished among the mean streets. What you can do, in your private, inner being, is remain unmoved by what you must do to redeem society; indeed, you must remain unmoved, lest you could not redeem society because, no longer being private, you would be part of society. The circular argument, in its commitment to the notion that "rude wit" and "a lively sense of the grotesque" will save you from being tarnished, is peculiarly American. Here is the subject—the American dream, tarnished, defended—though, as in all sound acts of deceit, it remains unstated.

The apparent beginning, therefore, actually arises at the second stage-stop on the journey: asking the right question. Most detective stories are posed as discrete questions: Who killed Cock Robin? Who took the pearls? What is the Musgrave ritual? Who purloined the letter? What caused the victim to fall—was he pushed? Since children can think of an infinitude of questions, reasonable adults will have no difficulty in reshaping the world in terms of questions asked by detectives. However, these questions must have certain characteristics about them if they are to shape a story, in the same sense that the historian who tells a story, the lawyer who reconstructs a story, the doctor who follows a story back to root cause, must share certain definable characteristics that encompass rules. The question must be capable of being interpreted; if the answer is truly rather than supposedly evident, one has a catechism in hand, not a question. The question must have an answer, or several answers. The question must not be limited to a hidden statement of fact. And the question must fit the needs and talents of the questioner: at base it must be autobiographical. It was of this last need that Chandler was speaking, even if romantically, when he wrote of the man "who is not himself mean" but who must be at home with sham, pettiness, and lies.

The question must be capable of containing a truth. It must be significant in that we must think it matters to have the answer. It must be interesting, for though everyone is entitled to feel that even a conversation with one's own murderer lacks interest, no one is without a definition of the interesting: oneself. When Edmund Wilson told us that he did not care who killed Roger Ackroyd, he told us more about himself than he knew.

Having established the question—usually by posing a crime that moves throughout the novel as metaphor for the question—the writer of detective fiction may then proceed along the formulaic paths of expectation. The other stages essential to the formula, though they need not follow rigidly the order of inherent logic, are: showing the finding of evidence to provide the data upon which an answer to the question may be posed; evaluating the evidence so that each item takes on a weighted value of its own; organizing the evidence so that one may begin to detect a pattern of cause and effect; submitting the evidence to the reader for its credibility; providing the evidence with a context that enlarges and confuses the meanings to be placed upon the elements under interrogation; and finally reviewing the evidence with the reader, in the older detective story (as in Ellery Queen) quite literally so, in the contemporary form largely by indirection. At each of these stages, the subtext will, in our times, arise from a series of moral questions, as in the nineteenth century the subtext pointed toward a world based upon whatever rational system by which the irrational might be made tolerable prevailed at the time: the Enlightenment, Darwinian evolution, or the belief that the wretched of the streets would always be with us. As in chemistry, a "solution" emerges from the process, which is, despite all attempts at obfuscation, in the end seen to be orderly, rational, scientific, even mechanical once understood. "Elementary, my dear Watson."

This is the formula, and as "tough" as the modern detective story is said to be, it is at base reassuring, sentimental, nostalgic, manipulative. And why not? Do we not say of much great literature that it is read the better to understand ourselves, humankind, nature, the world, in explanation of the ways of God to man? Making sense of an apparently disorderly universe that visits plague, pestilence, famine, and flood upon the chosen is the subject of what we customarily regard as our greatest literature. The tension between order and subversion of our hope for order, the manipulation of the art of the false confession, the leap of faith from inference to fact upon which we act— these are basic to learning a tolerance for complexity, to finding laughter in frustration, to the experience of joy in humanity.

"Toughness" is, after all, a matter of taste. In Roman Polanski's crime film, *Chinatown*, Faye Dunaway admits to incest with her father, and dies after suggesting to Jack Nicholson that the thought is "too tough" for him to take. In Gilbert Keith Chesterton's often-praised short stories, there are gratuitous racial remarks that are certainly, by today's standards, offensive. One suspects that the only reason Ronald Knox did not include among his decalogue a rule to the effect that the detective may not be a homosexual is that the thought did not occur to him, but today

Joseph Hansen can create, in Dave Brandstetter, a figure Mickey Spillane would have dismissed as a faggot. In such adjustments to society's expectations detective fiction reflects our concerns, and at times demarks the outer limits of our tolerance.

Nor is this formula limited to the West, though it began in Western Europe and remains very much the product of high-technology, scientific societies. If the British and Americans dominate the field, the Swedes, French, and Germans have made significant contributions; so, too, of course, have Canadians, Australians, and, in Dame Ngaio Marsh, a New Zealander. Yet one finds the genre adaptable to other societies as they too begin to be caught up in the problems of the higher technology. The Soviet Union has its crime writers even though it does not admit to crime, and in Japan such authors as Akimitsu Takagi and Kobo Abe have written straightforward procedural mysteries and surreal detective stories in the manner of Borges. Edogawa Rampo, a phonetic pseudonym meant to speak of Edgar Allan Poe, wrote short stories in the rationalistic manner of Poe. Lim Thean Soo in Singapore and Manohar Malgonkar in India provide us with spy-thriller mysteries that read nearly as well as the average such tale published in New York. Indeed, the genre appears to have few geographical limitations: Ivo Muscat-Azzopardi has produced Bendu Muskat, the Maltese detective, while O. Llew. Rowlands and W. T. Williams give us Nansi'r Dditectif. In Nigeria Kole Omotoso, in *Fella's Choice* (1974), shows us Inspector Fella Dandogo battling against the dreaded BOSS, the South African Bureau of State Security, which seeks to subvert Nigerian stability.

Each of these "exotic" writers lends verisimilitude to the plot by careful attention to local detail, so that one senses the books emerging from their landscapes. None are anywhere nearly so good as Arthur Conan Doyle, though all attempt to emulate him, if not for his science, and not by supplying a nearly omniscient detective with a Watson figure, then by remembering that the story must be rooted in the texture of its time and place. (Here, again, is a substantial difference from much science fiction.) Doyle can be read by a child for the story alone, can be read by a teenager for a sense of construction, and can be read by an adult for his knowledge of why we are intrigued by those dogs that did not bark in our night. Even the professional historian may marvel at the skill with which so simple a matter as the incidental names of lesser characters is dealt with by the truly professional writer; for Doyle weaves into his tales casual references that his contemporaries would instantly have understood, by which substantial baggage is shipped home free. The so-called unpublished Holmes cases, referred to by Watson from time to time as tales "for which the world was not yet prepared," hinted at horrors that scholars today must reconstruct but that were grasped at once by the readers of the time. Nicholas Meyer's *Seven Per Cent Solution* has brought into the open Doyle's references to Holmes's cocaine addiction, and has made public the subject of drug-taking in a way Doyle could not. Samuel Rosenberg has done even more to reveal how Holmesian allusions told his readers, and tell those of us who reconstruct the past, much about "the other Victorians," in a perfectly titled book, *Naked Is the Best Disguise*. This is especially so when technology can provide us with so many disguises, leading to the temptation to abandon the purity of the formula for intellectual gadgetry.

The formula was well stated by the poet W. H. Auden in his essay "The Guilty Vicarage." Simply: "a murder occurs; many are suspected; all but one suspect, who is the murderer, are eliminated; the murderer is arrested or dies." Auden went on to argue that the classic formula required a closed society "so that the possibility of an outside murderer (and hence of the society being totally innocent) is excluded." The closed society means that, among friends, if one is a murderer at least that one is deceitful, and into the garden of Eden, or "the Great Good Place," one has introduced evil. Auden thought Chandler quite wrong to give murder back to those who did it well, for professional killers were obtrusions from outside, from "the Great Wrong Place," and stories focused on their motivations, which are obvious, were studies of a criminal milieu rather than detective stories.

Auden posed for the modern detective story precisely the tension with which it deals best, though he chose to exclude rather than include half the real question: Why are there professional killers? Apart from the psychological question, a traditional detective story may still focus on the skilled professional, since Auden's definition of mystery may be served by the question, Who hired the killer? Who chose deliberately to bring the Great Wrong Place into the tidy world of the Great Good Place? Anyone choosing to negate life was, Auden thought, claiming omnipotence, and he who claims omnipotence is by definition a rebel against Eden. It is on the bridge between the Great Good and the Great Wrong places that so much of modern crime fiction takes place, for Auden's initial definition, though morally sound, is unsound in an immoral world: the child watching the innocent hanged in *The Ox-Bow Incident* has learned that all the suspects save one, who is the murderer, are not eliminated, and that the murderer neither is arrested nor dies. In *Falling Angel*, for example, William Hjortsberg slowly brings both the reader and the detective to the realization that, unknown to the detective, he is the murderer, cunningly giving to the cliché "private eye" a meaning that verges on the occult. Ending on Palm Sunday, the novel includes a black sex figure named Epiphany and a villain, Cyphre, who apparently is Satan. The detective, Angel, leads Epiphany—who turns out to be his daughter, though he discovers this long after he has slept with her— to her death, his gun thrust into her vagina.

Now this is as close to moral pornography as "a novel" is likely to get; certainly it is "too tough" by any definition of the term. Yet Hjortsberg's mad journey through the clichés of "the hard-boiled dick" shows us as clearly as any book can both how permissive detective fiction can be, all discussion of the formulaic notwithstanding, and how much distance there is between the golden age of detective fiction and today, a distance nonetheless easily traversed by the logic of Auden's argument, if one sets aside his restrictive definition. Auden's own logic brought him to see that detective fiction was akin to fantasy, however "realistic" its details, for it supposed an original innocence, a Garden, against which could be measured the magnitude of evil. The actual fantasy is the notion that one may escape back to such a Garden, while one must face away from the Garden never to return. Auden thus saw detective fiction as the Christian morality play restated in modern dress.

If this is so—and I believe it is—the question of guilt becomes central, and where guilt must be determined, and when determined weighed, the problem of evidence arises once again. Hence the meticulous stages through which detective fiction—whether of the golden age, in which the stages are clear and sequential, or of today, in which they are quite unclear and apparently oftentimes random—must carry the reader, or the reader carry the fiction. If this is a formula, it is the broadest conceivable one, embracing all literature.

[95]

Detective fiction thus leads us to reconsider our values. The various visions of hell provided by such fiction are no less varied than those given us by the great painters of the past who sought to show precisely what torments lay ahead. In the Middle Ages it was accepted that places of retribution both existed and could be visited by the stout of heart who sought out the proper path, returning with a fuller knowledge of man's future. Literature and art tell of these journeys, and Bosch and others depicted the scene at the end of the voyage. These descents into hell, to the center of the earth, to Lucifer's lair, were generally secular in spirit though churchly in intent; in their narrative detail they were the pornography of their time. Such a romance as *Huon d'Auvergne* takes the reader through rivers teeming with serpents; past devils fighting among themselves who might, if distracted, fall upon the travelers; to places of great clamor, where figures are dragged behind horses to their eternal pain. In short, a typical weekend with Arthur Lyons in Los Angeles. In this journey the reader was meant to think again of his life; in modern detective fiction, one is cast against walls indifferent to one's views, until those views, tested, are comfortably reconfirmed in a world rendered once again orderly, or are destroyed. (There is a compelling analysis of *Huon d'Auvergne* in D.D.R. Owen's *Vision of Hell*. The most intriguing vision met on the journey is at "the fifth gate," the abode of the Seven Liberal Arts, where the occupant is condemned to "a continual chanting of his knowledge" [Edinburgh, 1970, p. 187].)

Earlier I spoke of William Haggard, and of how he challenged the limousine liberals of his native land. Surely R. L. Gordon, in *The River Grows Wider*, which concerns itself with a rising, and admirable, political star who is destroyed by an act we are never certain he committed, has forced every reader who encounters him to think again about his own principles under stress. Writers such as P. D. James, Sheila Radley, Reginald Hill, Michael Innis, and Dick Francis persistently raise questions that reflect such evidence of ourselves as we have been able to gather, about honesty, duty, courage, and all those virtues some satirize by invoking the Boy Scouts, though all of us must deal with them. One's reactions change, of course, and no one writer will be received conventionally by all: "The Fall of the House of Usher" may be replete with symbols of incest, though readers still puzzling over whether Washington did cut down the cherry tree are unlikely to notice the symbols. "The Murders in the Rue Morgue," read in a day when all of us have been trained to visualize the actions of which we read, is hideously gruesome—far more so, in fact, than in its own day, when the visual image came less easily to readers not already exposed to the daily fix of violence from tabloid newspaper photographs and from television. Surely our view of Sayers's *Gaudy Night* is, in part, reshaped as our own position in society, or views on the feminist movement, or anti-semitism, change. One's third reading of Faulkner, Dickens, or Borges is unlikely to lead to the same conclusions as one's first reading.

The trends so evident in detective fiction are at once reflections of society, creators of change in us as readers, and accurate statements about the relations between societies. Snobbery is accompanied, as one critic remarked, with more violence, since in a world shaped by the language of Marx, snobbery put into practice is an extreme form of violence. Detective fiction is far more overtly political today, following the trend first established by Eric Ambler when he carried the spy thriller into the anticapitalist camp. Sex is more explicit, as it is in our lives, so that the band of readers who genuinely thought detective fiction was "escape literature" find that there is (as in fact there always has been) no escape within the literature. The detective is as world-weary as the spy, betrayed by society—by fellow policemen, by employers who lie about their real intent, by courts and politicians and priests—and through sentiment, also a betrayer of society, which wants the detective to clean up its garbage for it. Privacy of motive, like privacy for sex, does not exist—must not be allowed to exist.

Broadly speaking, detective fiction falls into three camps: the classic puzzle, which flourished during the golden age, at which Christie and Sayers were so good; the "hard-boiled dick," a private eye, quintessentially American, which we associate most immediately with Chandler; and the "procedural" story, usually about policemen at work as a team within the constraints and supporting mechanisms of an institutional framework, begun in England by Maurice Proctor and in the United States by Lawrence Treat, Ed McBain, and Hillary Waugh. All three of these camps share the characteristics espoused by Auden and taken up in the post-Auden extension of his argument: all move through the eight or so stages I have outlined; all use pungent imagery, hard words to hide the sentimentality at the core, letting a wisecrack cover the doubts one encounters on the journey; and all, by virtue of taking us on that journey through the stages of evidence-collecting and evaluation, focus on means rather than ends. They appear, then, to be anti-ideological, the ends being simply the restoring of order by producing a "solution," and ironic by virtue of the tension they induce between innocence and reality, expectation and performance, masquerade and respect for "the facts."

As we did with spy and thriller fiction, let us look briefly at one subset of detective fiction: the hard-boiled school. While primarily American, the school has had its English exponents, of whom James Hadley Chase is perhaps the best known. Still, *No Orchids for Miss Blandish* is to detective fiction what Faulkner's *Sanctuary* is to southern regional literature: misleading. The hard-boiled egg, despite some imitators, is basically all-American.

The formula was set by Hammett, Chandler, and Ross Macdonald. The Western moves to the city; behind the facade of toughness is someone sentimental enough to care about both truth and people, though truth comes first; dialogue is used to reveal character, and character is used to motivate plot; the reader is steadily pushed to the limit of that which he will find too tough, in language, situation, visual image; a quiet competence stands revealed behind a shabby exterior. Forty bucks a day and expenses buys the expertise but never the person. Chandler patented the formula in *The Big Sleep* (1939) and most especially in his masterpiece, *The Lady in the Lake* (1943). Kenneth Millar, as he became Ross Macdonald, extended the formula, and within their different locales and the speech patterns of those locales, John D. MacDonald, Charles Williams, and Robert Knowlton replicated it. MacDonald hit his stride in 1963 (*The Drowner*) and 1964 (*The Deep Blue Goodbye*); Williams, in *The Catfish Tangle*, and Knowlton, in *Court of Crows*, substituted bourbon and hominy grits for the muscatel and faded orange groves of southern California.

Once established, the formula is so attractive to those who like it that imitation becomes the highest form of art: to be hailed as "the new Ross Macdonald" is the highest praise. Eight writers in particular have stepped into that select company, every one having been compared by one critic or another, perhaps in search of a reference point that those little versed in what hard-boiled dicks do with their time might recognize, to either Macdonald or Chandler. In general these writers are so much alike, yet so good, one may simply mention them, though in truth they fall into three rough groupings. There are those who write mild parodies of the style, inoffensive enough not to turn away those in search of another Chandler, yet with a wise-ass voice of their own: Roger L. Simon, whose Moses Wine in *Wild Turkey* combines the muscatel and bourbon as implied; Andrew Bergman, who from *The Big Kiss Off of 1944* has developed his own special area, the Chandler pastiche set in the Chandler times (Stuart Kaminsky tries this, less well); and Michael Z. Lewin, who, through his series figure Albert Samson, shows how to *Ask the Right Question* and *The Way We Die Now*, at least in Indiana. Lewin is the mildest of the parodists, though the frequently aimless talk in which Samson engages is both authentically boring and an exact recapitulation of the Marlowe wise-crack as it would have truly been said by a less literary figure.

The second group consists of the direct imitators, who appear to have studied the structure, pace, and language of Chandler to the point that they are his echo. Charles Alverson is the most explicit about this, for in his *Goodey's Last Stand* (1975) he stages an actual laying on of hands, a passing of the torch from a Marlowe figure to the next generation as represented by Goodey, who is *Not Sleeping, Just Dead*, as his sentiments unfold to us in a subsequent book. Timothy Harris, in *Kyd for Hire*, provides just that level of wisecrack that speaks of imitation: "You want to solve a crime, Granville? Why don't you go arrest your tailor?" And Lawrence Block, in creating a series figure, Matt Scudder (and then apparently abandoning him for a verbose, and singularly silly, burglar-turned-detective,

Bernie Rhodenbarr), apparently proved too tough for his readers, who did not materialize. Even so, on my short list of underappreciated writers, I would place Block high for three of the most effective transfers of the Chandler method into the milieu of New York City: *The Sins of the Fathers, In the Midst of Death,* and *Time to Murder and Create.*

Apart from these imitators, because better, out of the same stable and now racing on their own fast tracks, are Robert B. Parker, whose series figure, Spenser, not only lives in Boston but likes it, and Arthur Lyons. Parker's Spenser thinks he is a gourmet, though Fritz would not have let him into the kitchen in his brownstone, for he uses catsup and makes his own omelets, badly if one is to believe the recipes (like Wolfe, he likes his beer); he also thinks he is tough, which he is. He is well-read and hides it, and he respects women for themselves and not for how he will use them or what he wants them to be. Starting in *The Godwulf Manuscript* in 1973, through *Mortal Stakes* (1975), the best detective story ever written with a baseball setting, to *Promised Land* (1976), which belongs with *Gaudy Night* on the shelf of women's liberationist literature, to *Early Autumn* (1981), which is about forms of maturity, Parker has grown in stature to the point that he has set in train his own imitators.

Somewhere moving across Parker's path, then, yet remaining in California, as bitter as Block, as close to parody as Lewin, as consciously imitative as Alverson, yet closest of all to Parker, so that together they comprise my small, loose collectivity, is Arthur Lyons. Most consciously it is the mid-passage Ross Macdonald that Lyons pursues. His detective, Jacob Asch, is Jewish, and this is frequently relevant, setting him apart from Sam Spade, Marlowe, and Archer. In *The Dead are Discreet* (1974) he explores

Jesus freaks, in *All God's Children* (1975) a motorcycle gang. As Chandler worked the posh estates above Wilshire Boulevard, Lyons works their children and grandchildren, driven to the alternative culture by their parents' affluence. They, too, have fallen out of *The High Window*.

8

DEATH, hell, anguish, deceit—these are the constant themes of literature and art. So are compassion, resurrection, joy, and truth. Mirror images reflect their opposites, and if detective fiction holds a mirror to society and gives back a reflection of its fears, it also implies the presence of those qualities that are missing. Such fiction is not "depressing" save thinking makes it so; in any event, manic depression implies highs as well as lows. Even amid the sleaze of Arthur Lyons, as in *Hard Trade*, there is the promise that all conditions encompass their opposites, just as in *Castles Burning* Lyons uses the familiar theme of family despair to suggest what might have been. Reading detective fiction may, to some, seem much like visiting the Munch-Museet in Oslo, where one confronts one after another the versions Edvard Munch gave to *The Scream*; but to others, able to see the greater range both of the fiction and of Munch, the more representative work may well be *Evening on Karl Johan Street*, with its gaunt depiction of anonymity, or *Puberty*, which speaks of the connection between death and sexuality through a girl's body. Both these paintings imply the *possibility* of their opposite, of identity, growth, and serenity, even though neither Munch nor detective fiction achieves that opposite. The truly good writer of detective fiction will make us aware of issues of which we would rather remain unaware, bootlegging onto our shelves the literature of cathartic subversion.

It is generally recognized that one reason people read detective fiction is for catharsis. Indeed, Ronald Knox, whom I have somewhat abused previously here, wisely made the point that true catharsis is not best achieved by a mystery. Writing in praise of the Father Brown cycle of stories by G. K. Chesterton, which he found to be "something more" than detective stories, Knox first satirized the frequently cited reason why such stories are popular: "it may be reasonably maintained that a detective story is meant to be read in bed, by way of courting sleep; it ought not to make us think—or rather, it ought to be a kind of *catharsis*, taking our minds off the ethical, political, theological problems which exercise our waking hours by giving us artificial problems to solve instead." But these are not, as Knox then remarked, artificial problems, and Chesterton "smuggles into our minds, under the disguise of a police mystery, the very solicitudes he was under contract to banish." Thus the very form of the mystery is itself a deceit, and one that we welcome.

Jorge Luis Borges, master Argentinean writer, poses mysteries more obliquely, tantalizingly, perhaps obscurely. Yet "Death and the Compass" and "Tlon, Uqbar, Orbis Tertius" (both of which appear in his *Ficciones*) are examples of the two subcategories of the genre that we have examined briefly in this essay: the first, however hidden, is a moral/procedural tale; the second speaks to the sense of mirror-menace so central to spy fiction, since it presupposes the existence of a secret organization that is spreading either true knowledge or, more likely, fictitious impressions, which when accepted will change the entirety of man's recording of his activity on earth. Having initiated this mystery, Borges poses a truly central question, since the presupposition itself is not false to any body, institution, organization, church, or political party committed to a fundamentally messianic point of view. The question is, How will, and how ought, such an organization proceed? From this question flows a counterfactual analysis that is, surely, factual in the sense of being utterly logical to the presupposition.

Mystery and detection go together within the genre, the first posing and the second resolving the "problem." The detection must adhere to the world as presupposed by the mystery, so the procedures of deduction are circumscribed by the definition of the mystery itself. For this reason some critics have thought detective fiction so formulaic as to be conservative in mode as well as in ethical message and less capable of growth than other forms of fiction. I do not see why this need be so, provided one focuses not on the second but on the first element in the construction, the mystery as posed. As Sir Thomas Browne wrote, "All things are artificial, for nature is the art of God." That is, the artificiality said to limit mystery fiction is an open invitation to create art. To be donnish for a moment and dot the page with quotations, let Keats do for us what we cannot do for ourselves, with his concept of negative capability: "that is, when a man is capable of being in uncertainties, mysteries, doubts, without any irritable reaching after face and reason." The mystery provides us with this capability, for while the central "problem" may be satisfactorily resolved, in that the murderer is uncovered and, perhaps, justice is done, with a form of catharsis achieved for some, many mysterious elements relating to precise actions and precise motivations at precise times, as opposed to general explanations of motive, will almost certainly and properly be left unresolved. In P. D. James's *Innocent Blood* we "know" why the figures have acted as they have, in the sense that in Ross Macdonald's work we are eventually informed as to the motivational linkages between individuals and the events they create. But in none of these works are we shown precisely why the individuals chose to act precisely as they did, rather than in some other manner sufficiently different in form to have allowed for a different sequence of cause and effect. That is, the formal puzzle is "solved," the "detective" does his or her job, while the mystery of human choice is left in a condition of complex plausibility, so that even the tidiest of endings remains, upon reflection, ambiguous. Indeed, as the father of modern conservatism remarked (I speak of Edmund Burke), "Where mystery begins [that is, remains truly unresolved], justice ends."

The detective is invoked less to explain than to show the mystery, to be one or two reflective steps ahead of us. Even that most mysterious of texts, the Bible, declared, "Behold, I *show* you a mystery"; the detective, whether Renaissance explorer, psychiatrist, or Philip Marlowe / Lew Archer, in seeking to discover matters artfully concealed becomes an instrument for detecting that which may escape our attention, society's early-warning device to suggest when abnormalities may be taken as normative. If one turns to the dictionary one learns that detecting means "to uncover, lay bare, expose; to find out, or to discover the presence, existence, or fact of something apt to elude notice." That which is apt to elude notice changes from period to period and society to society; the Confession "wherein men do detect their sins" changes in function in a post-Freudian age and in content as sins themselves are taken to change. In the end, one is detecting shades of meaning, and the literature that does this best—Dorothy Sayers in *Nine Tailors*, for example, if given a chance and a half by the alert reader—is as nuanced as the finest French prose.

But "to detect" once had other meanings as well, and while they are rendered archaic by the authority of the dictionary, detective fiction in its inherent conservatism retains these older meanings: "to display, to accuse, to discover a person *being*." P. D. James's *Cover Her Face* draws upon John Webster's *Duchess of Malfi* (c. 1614) to discover a person in the act of being: "Cover her face; mine eyes dazzle; she died young. / I think not so; her infelicity Seem'd to have years too many." We then, through the eyes of Detective Chief-Inspector Adam Dalgliesh, sometime poet, play Bosola to the reader's Ferdinand to discover both the who and the why behind the murder of Sally Jupp, whose name carries us back to the Dickens Miss James so admires. Bearing the seeds of ruin in themselves, the figures in James ultimately detect their own beings, upon which follows their own destruction. "We shall not all sleep, but shall all be changed." The artifice of the false confession becomes a statement about the self-deceptions we all entertain.

In the end, then, detective fiction is, as suggested, like history in yet another way: it is autobiographical in the moral dimension. In the choice of subject matter and method of approach to subject, the historian draws upon autobiography. In the genuine mystery, and indeed in the most cunningly crafted of the thrillers, detection becomes self-detection. Consider one of the most inconsistent yet most significant figures within the genre, Geoffrey Household. Here is a craftsman who has written several excessively bad books (*Arabesque, Olura, Red Anger*) punctuated by three works of the highest talent: *Rogue Male* (one of his earliest, in 1939); *Watcher in the Shadows* (1960), from which I have taken a subtheme of my argument; and *Dance of the Dwarfs* (1968). These three works are a continuum in which the hunter becomes the hunted, and then once again the hunter, and (in the final novel) yet again the hunted. The constant shift in actual point of view, despite the apparent consistency of vision through first-person narrative, brilliantly reminds one of the parallels between research and detection. In *Rogue Male* the protagonist attempts to assassinate a European dictator who, given the year, most likely is Hitler; the attempt fails—no counterfactual history here—and the "hero" is pursued by the enemy to his own territory in Dorset, where he literally goes to ground in the Buchan tradition, hiding in a hole in the earth, reverting to the elemental animal. By doing so he throws off his pursuers and again becomes the hunter, once again on the path of assassination. Since the target is broadly hinted to be Hitler, we approve, both then, in 1939, and now in hindsight. Yet read the book today and turn the Rogue Male into a German and the target into a Churchill; for the ease with which hunter and hunted interchange suggests in the end the truly most effective counterfactual means of argumentation, and through argument, of explanation.

Household is explaining, not alone that things are not what they seem, but that only those who brave the dangers of steady, draining pursuit, of inquiry and doubt, will comprehend the mystery of their own resources. In *Watcher in the Shadows* we learn what it is to feel watched. At one level, the book functions rather as a didactic exercise on how the subject of a biographer must feel, as the hunted; at another level, we sense how behavior is modified because of the actuality or simply the perception of being watched, hunted, the object of inquiry; and on yet another level, we discover how the watcher responds, is changed by the act of watching. It is not pretentious to say that Household, in these two novels, has gone some distance toward posing the central dilemma of the biographer: how to be the hunter without becoming the hunted, the self-hunted through the autobiographical act of self-discovery as one sees oneself through the eyes of another. *Dance of the Dwarfs* thus completes this almost unconscious trilogy, in which a watcher most rational—a scientist, observing the flora and fauna of a remote South American region—slowly becomes aware that he is watched, and that all his science will not explain, and by not explaining will not protect, the world he thought so orderly. In shedding scientific rationality, Household's scientist dies, preserving his integrity. Some may find the resolution to *Dance of the Dwarfs* trite, though once read backwards against the mounting, undifferentiated evidence of the conclusion to come, and in the context of an alleged preface supplied by those who have sought to verify the journal that, like Poe's "MS Found in a Bottle," may be, by virtue of just three or four sentences, open to doubts that virtually strangle any absolute conclusion, the book captures the dilemma of the historian, the teller of history, the person responsible—in our continuum from cause through guilt—for the story of the past, the omnipresent detective. The book is brilliant, allusive, elusive, a rosary corresponding to the mysteries of redemption.

Can we dismiss such literature because it is "popular fiction," a "best-seller," a "vicarious stimulus"? George Eliot once dismissed popular fiction as "spiritual gin," perhaps because of the alleged happiness of the endings of much that was most popular. Whether gin truly induces a happy ending one might best leave to Hogarth, or to the mysteries of Eliot's intent. But surely were she writing today, George Eliot would not dismiss Household, or Chandler, or Lawrence Block, or even Agatha Christie in this manner, for her strictures apply appropriately only to those books that titillate to no moral, that are simply the intellectual equivalent of a fast fix, a roller-coaster ride, or are an allusive style with no point, the "new journalism." The variety of books about nasty babies (*Rosemary's Baby*), nasty fish (*Jaws*), bears, insects, birds, nasty dildos, nasty-nasty, is no more to be confused with the serious fiction of fun so well represented by Christie and (in the sense that self-discovery is, however hard to take, also joy) Household than are the modern bodice-ripping multivolume series of novels about Kentuckians, Westering, Aliens in space, and Thorn Birds to be compared with the virtually offstage deflowering of Tess by which we experience an effect upon all victims chosen merely because they are beautiful. The power of blackness is something far more powerful than the simple power to frighten.

Why does, or should, the detective/mystery story appeal, then? For as many reasons as there are individuals to whom it appeals, of course, as well as for the greater glory of God. But in an analytical age one must have a catalogue of reasons, a word that always suggests the reasonable, and often conjures up the unstated supportive word *good* reasons. We already have catalogued several "reasons" by way of rational explanation. Such literature fulfills our need for catharsis. It finally speaks to a sense of order. It poses moral problems in ways by which we may more comfortably stalk them. It conforms to Enlightenment values, Burkean expectations, and the libido. It speaks to our scientific consciousness, that deduction, observation properly understood, the development of general laws of behavior, and the application of technology will provide answers to our questions in the end. It suggests that the end, death, is as we were taught in a more religious age, for just as man, the only species to bury its dead under the original presumption of a return to life in some form, denies that death is definitive, man also sees death as part of a cycle of meaning; the mystery "explains" death in functional terms. Yet mystery fiction leaves room for a hint of the occult, and the door is wide open to ambiguity. In its form it is deceitful, so that form and function support the same end. And, let us admit it, detective fiction also entertains—not merely entertains, but significantly, delightfully, suffocatingly, desperately entertains. It is fun, seriously expressed, like Vivaldi, like Mozart before *Don Giovanni*, like Pete Seeger and the organ in Saint-Saëns.

And why, then, do we study such fiction? Partially because it is there, and today we study everything. Partially because it does represent society, though whether it speaks of fears not made real, of hard realities, or of the order for which society yearns, no one agrees. Partially, again, because it is fun. Broadly, however, the growing body of serious critics of detective fiction fall into two categories (leaving aside those who write gushingly for the "fanzines," devoting much space to plot summaries and instant value judgments on their favorite heroes). The first is the sociological: those who, interested in the popularity and growing sales of crime fiction, use the fiction to ask questions about society, sometimes comparatively between countries though most commonly within a single country. This group argues that the application of critical, literary skills to such fiction distorts its real function, since the canons of literary criticism generally look inward to the text in a way that can be appreciated by, and more important, is useful in revealing the assumptions of, only an educated minority. The more complicated the cultural artifact,* the happier the literary critic, and the more abstracted from any genuine understanding of precisely how detective fiction functions in society he becomes. On occasion the sociological approach is overtly, and more often vaguely, Marxist, in that it argues that "dominant cultures" (for which read the literary establishment) greet detective (and science) fiction with ignorance, contempt, and more insidiously, containment and pleas for dismissal. Thus the shape of detective fiction is actually determined by the desire of the middle and upper middle classes to have objects of disdain—ethnics, criminals, the working class, crime-ridden environments—so that the dominant group may continue to pass judgment on popular culture.†

There is, of course, some truth here, as there usually is in sociological argumentation, though the more useful truths are the more obvious ones. Certainly procedural detective fiction assures us that the careful following of the rule book will, in the end, produce results; the procedural school also reassures us that many cops are on the take, that crime is a dirty little matter and not one of bodies found in libraries, and that everyone, even Steve Carella of the 87th Precinct, Riverharb, Isola, makes stupid mistakes. But the sociological school misses its target because of its need to build general theories. McBain is often said to be a fascist, an intense conservative intent upon justifying all the nuance put into the phrase "law and order" by a

---

* This view is best represented by Stephen Knight in *Form and Ideology in Crime Fiction* (London, 1980), the work of an Australian scholar who specializes in Chaucer.
† This argument is most nakedly put by Gérard Klein in "A Petition by Agents of the Dominant Culture for the Dismissal of Science Fiction," in *Science-Fiction Studies*, VII (July, 1980). I apologize for the foolish inconsistency of drawing upon the hobgoblin of sci-fi.

Spiro Agnew. Perhaps; there is no doubt that he believes in capital punishment and summary justice for animals. But he also clearly recognizes that human beings *become* animals through a process; he apparently believes that the process might be changed, but he does not expect to reverse its effect upon those who have already undergone it. Those who hold McBain up as the arch-Republican of procedural fiction cannot have read *Hail to the Chief* (1973), a pointed, chilling, deceptively lucid attack on a gang leader who justifies immoral acts because he wanted to bring peace to the neighborhood: "I did it because I'm the president, that's why. I'm the elected leader, and it is my duty and my responsibility to take care of the people I am serving. That's all there is to it. That's all I got to say." The gang leader is certain of his morality: "I never killed nobody. I can also tell you that although I ordered the raids that ended the war once and for all—and don't forget I *did* end the war, the war *is* over, there's never going to be no more trouble in this neighborhood—it was not me personally who did any of the killing. . . . And if you look at just the blood, then you can forget the very real things I accomplished." Can anyone possibly not see the obvious, that this novel is about Richard Nixon, Watergate, the Cambodian bombings? Is this the work of an advocate of "law and order" as Agnew defined it? Of order, and the law, yes, and conservative in the sense that Edmund Burke understood, yes, but no fascist this.

Perhaps the sociological school finds writers like McBain "right wing" because they describe clinically what they see. This is part of the procedure, the technique, of seeing with the icicle in the eye. *Hail to the Chief* opens:

They found the bodies in an open ditch on the northernmost extreme of the 87th Precinct. . . . The

[112]

six bodies were lying in angular confusion on top of the mud-colored ice. There was another color staining the ice. The color was blood. The bodies were naked. Their nakedness made the night seem even colder than it was. . . . There were three men, two young girls, and a baby in the ditch. The baby was clutched in the arms of one of the girls. Carella did not turn away until he saw the baby.

In the procedural story, you get what you see. The mystery is not hidden by the words, for the intent of the artist is to use an entire squad room as the hero, a composite portrait of men embedded in an organization, of organizational man at work, triumphing through care, effort, weary repetition: through procedure. For this reason dialogue plays an important part in McBain's novels. Entire chapters consist of nothing but dialogue, much of it irrelevant (and clearly so at the time), the function of which is to strengthen the awareness of a procedure embedded within the system of a squad, a family by which the men come to know each other, and later, through the knowing, may work effectively together, and by the book, to a conclusion. Yet almost always chance plays a rôle, and if genius consists of the prepared mind, then the solution to the mystery in a McBain book arises from the observant policeman who grasps the meaning of an accident; for seldom does detection in the normal sense of the word take place in procedural fiction. This, too, is surely true, for if it is realism we seek, we must realize how often policework must wait, depending on the lucky break, the informer, the simultaneity of chance occurrences.

Why this should be seen in a Marxist mode, or as particularly speaking to the urban condition (Hillary Waugh's Fred Fellows works his procedural paces in a recognizable small town, actually Guilford, Connecticut), or as proof of the validity of a sociological approach, is difficult to tell. Of McBain one such critic says that "the consumerist source and liberal individualist basis of empiricism" stand revealed. Possibly so, though the historian in us must never forget to ask, And So What? The social approach to analysis remains valuable, for rather like procedural detective fiction, by a fortuitous connection of accidents, it does from time to time tell us something we would not have seen for ourselves. Stephen Knight, for example, discovers in Raymond Chandler an elitist point of view, from which the poor and blacks do not attract his attention. Chandler's views are those of the educated middle class, he finds. This is scarcely surprising, since Chandler had been educated at Dulwich College in England and was of the middle class, as were his readers; the poor, and blacks, were not generally buying detective fiction when *Farewell, My Lovely* was published in 1940, and Chandler wrote to eat.* (It is surely more surprising that no one black appears in William Carlos Williams's long poem to an industrial city, Paterson.) Yet it may be useful to encounter the accidents of the sociological procedure, to be told that gossip functions in Agatha Christie virtually as an independent narrator (upon reflection, not surprising, since St. Mary Mead is a small town, yet one had not reflected), or that *Farewell, My Lovely* was originally to have been called "The Second Murderer" with intended reference to Richard III, a title the publisher, Knopf, rejected. Even so, to the historian—that is, to the detective in us attempting to comprehend the reality of detective fiction—this example

* Knight, *Form and Ideology*, pp. 135–66, on Chandler; the quotation on McBain is on p. 190.

[1 1 4]

seems deficient, for the unasked question is, Why would Chandler have allowed his publisher to change the title of his work? A part of the answer arises from the original date of publication, 1940; it was Chandler's second book, when the sociological reality was that he was not yet an established author and that he needed to conform to his publisher's sense of what would work best in the market. The sociologist does not comment on this fact, and, indeed, cites throughout a 1949 reprint edition of the text of *Farewell, My Lovely*, apparently unconcerned that by then Chandler had put *The High Window, The Lady in the Lake*, and *The Little Sister* behind him as well.

This is not to say that the sociological approach to popular culture is without its values. The sociology of knowledge is such that the approach itself is revealing of the uses to which another institution, academe, can put a body of writing. Very real questions of significance concerning issues of popular culture do arise,* and need to be addressed, though to date the need to validate theory appears to have overridden the need (as felt by detective/historian/literalist) to remain faithful to the text. The other approach, therefore, has advanced the study of mystery fiction somewhat farther, though not yet far enough: the case presented by literary modernists, structuralists, and the traditional literary critic. This body of writers is concerned with the inventiveness and the structure of detective fiction from within, with the text for itself. Some members of the guild, most notably Geoffrey Hartman, have written valuable essays on either specific writers or the larger body of

---

* I make a stab at some of these questions in my *Detective Fiction* (Englewood Cliffs, N.J., 1980) and "The Sinister Oriental: Thriller Fiction and the Asian Scene," in R. W. Winks and C. S. Gray, eds., *Asia in Western-Language Fiction* (forthcoming).

fiction, but for the most part criticism informed by the explanatory argumentation of Northrop Frye and those who followed, through Roland Barthes, the fashionable and impenetrable Derrida, to Paul de Man, has little to tell us about *No Orchids for Miss Blandish*. If a simple soul reads Frye's *Anatomy of Criticism* correctly, he believes that literature is impersonal, inward, self-contained, virtually without an artistic intent in the sense of a voice, to be heard from book to book as a growth in tenor, by which one can trace an originating first cause. History, detective fiction, and logic all believe that individuals are causes and that one must look outside the text, beyond the document, behind the fact, to understand first (in the sense of most nearly orginating) cause, so that the genre itself is, in form, anti-pathetic to the newer forms of criticism. Willful misreading is, surely, induced, and is this not what Christie did to Edmund Wilson?

The body of critical literature thus depends more than is good for the genre upon amateurs, like this one, and upon those who stray into the field temporarily from philosophy, religion, comparative literature, or on occasion from the far side of the moon, straightforwardly explicative English criticism. Good work has been offered up by Robert Champigny, Erik Routley, John Cawelti, and George Grella. Good work too comes from those who, as practitioners of the craft, seek to analyze what it is that they do: Ross Macdonald, John Ball, Robert Barnard (on Christie), Anthony Boucher, and perhaps foremost Julian Symons. The adventurer from afar, such as Jacques Barzun, continues to make contributions of importance, especially in providing categories for argumentation, wry and witty ripostes to more self-consciously serious colleagues, and the occasional romp through the history of how the Whodunit became the How- or Whydunit.* This lively, if academically unestablished, body of analysis does not generally qualify as literary criticism, and such writers as Symons are consigned to the back of the book in the same manner as the literature they examine. The vigilantes in the field either choose the wrong strategy—the high road—or choose the right strategy and execute it badly—the low road, as traveled by most.

This is to our good fortune. Most subjects have been studied to death. There are on my shelves perhaps a thousand crime novels I have kept because I thought them worth keeping; far more have been left behind in railway cars and in airport lounges. If Ross Thomas and Ed McBain and Robert Parker don't become too self-conscious from having too much written about them, they may just go on writing, and I may need space for another thousand crime novels on my shelves before I reach Stanley Ellin's Dreadful Summit. As long as one remains a historian, one will need that icicle in the eye. As long as Peter Shaffer continues to write plays, I will wonder whether, as in *Amadeus*, we have been exploring the mystery of mediocrity, or some other text altogether. (*Did* Shaffer read Pushkin? *Did*

---

* I am particularly fond of Jacques Barzun's work, perhaps because he is a historian, but I do wish he did not feel the need to put all the horses into stalls so that they might eat his hay. I think he is wrong to argue that the short story is an ideal form for detective fiction, since there is little opportunity in the short form to obfuscate plot and draw out the resultant moral ambiguities. The short story is, in essence, bound to the puzzle form, which seems to me the most nearly sterile of all the subforms of the genre. In *The Delights of Detection* (New York, 1961), Barzun finds five parts to the ideal short story: the preamble, the predicament, the discourse on method, the action arising from the deduction, and the explanation. This seems to me not so. But then, I have already argued that I have eight horses (and then fitted them to nine stalls, if the reader was counting).

Salieri kill Mozart?) There is still hope that one body of serious fun may go on being both serious and fun. Why still hug the dear deceit? Were all precisely as it seems, how dreary a world. We still have to ask the right question, interrogate our environment, challenge the received wisdom, and take pleasure in knowing that we are large, we contain multitudes, we contradict ourselves. Detective fiction creates for us an anonymity; within it, we may constitute the last law on earth, at the freezing point, making decisions (to be "proved" right or wrong) as we go, responsible for them, tricked, disappointed, triumphant, joyful, honest as to our mistakes, setting the record straight. As we make leaps of faith between evidence and decision in our daily lives—to board this bus, to choose that doctor, to add these pounds—so we make leaps of faith between evidence and conclusion, through the public historiography and the private autobiography that are the literature we read, and in the reading re-create, as James predicted, the watcher-without now the self-aware and thus self-watched. We learn how to define evidence, to use up our intellectual shoe leather in pursuit of an operable truth, to take joy from the receding horizon and pleasure in the discovery that the answer has not yet been found, that there is more work to be done. We reaffirm our belief that people matter, for their individual, discrete actions are causes, embraced within yet separable from those great collectivities of causation, the century's isms, by which the simple and the truly corrupt would explain life. We learn that what people believe to be true is as important as the objective truth defined by researcher/detective. In Marlowe and Archer we meet people who have no *use* for their conclusions, no desire for vengeance, who know that society will supply the uses while they may engage in the happy ambiguity of simply finding the facts, which, inert, take on life when embedded in a context of cause and effect. There is a continuity from Babar, and the Pie and the Patty-Pan, through Joseph Altsheler and John Buchan, to Household, C. P. Snow, Norman Mailer, and John Fowles. Is not *The French Lieutenant's Woman* a fine history? A superlative novel? A compelling mystery?

Ultimately one reads detective fiction because it involves judgments—judgments made, passed upon, tested. In raising questions about purpose, it raises questions about cause and effect. In the end, like history, such fiction appears to, and occasionally does, decode the environment; appears to and occasionally does tell one what to *do*; appears to and occasionally does set the record straight. Setting the record straight ought to matter. Detective fiction, in its high seriousness, is a bit like a religion, in pursuit of truths best left examined at a distance. As with all fine literature, history, philosophy, as with the written word wherever employed creatively, it can lead us to laughter in our frustration, to joy in our experience, and to tolerance for our complexities. It begins as Hawthorne so often does, and as the best of historians do, with a personal word, diffident, apparently modest, in search of the subject by asking (later, with Gertrude Stein), What is the question? It ends, as historians who have completed their journey often do, with an authoritative tone, the complex explained, the mystery revealed, the sequence made sensible in the true meaning of the word: tactile, *ars poetica,* "palpable and mute / As a globed fruit."

9

W ELL, I've told about three lies in this book,* one big and maybe two small. I suspect that's about right for a book on this subject. It's catching.

* This is another one. It depends on who you are, of course. Librarians don't call anything that runs to under a hundred pages in print a book. Publishers do. In the immortality sweepstakes librarians win, being the Big Definers; publishers are just the originating pushers. Some librarians won't even catalogue you if you can't say what you have to say in more than a hundred pages. Some places you wind up in a vertical file, which is kind of like being debriefed by someone who doesn't know what to ask. I hope the publisher puts all this on good thick paper, with wide margins; if I'm lucky and he's clever, he can get a hundred pages in print out of this. But he won't. [Ah, but he has. Librarians, please note. *Der Herausgeber.*]

Index

A

Abe, Kobo, 92
Acheson, Dean, 70
Ackroyd, Roger, 11, 27, 84, 90
Airport, 7
Allbeury, Ted, 63
All God's Children, 102
Allingham, Margery, 12, 37
Altsheler, Joseph, 24–27, 119
Alverson, Charles, 100
Amadeus, 117
The Amateur, 55, 58
Ambler, Eric, 53, 63, 65, 79, 97
Amis, Kingsley, 36
Anatomy of Criticism, 116
Andrews, Dana, 28
And Then There Were None, 62n
Angleton, James, 46
Another Crying Woman, 60
Antonioni, Michelangelo, 17
Arabesque, 107
Archer, Lew, 40, 101, 105, 118
The Arena, 77
Arendt, Hannah, 45
"Arrival of the Bee Box," 20–22
Asch, Jacob, 101

Ask the Right Question, 100
The Aspern Papers, 16
Assignment: Murder, 68
Auden, W. H., 93, 94, 95, 98
Austen, Jane, 77
Autry, Gene, 27, 28

B

Bagley, Desmond, 63, 65–66
Ball, John, 116
Barchester Towers, 81
Barnard, Robert, 37, 83, 116
Barthes, Roland, 11, 116
Barzun, Jacques, 34, 116, 117n
Beck, Martin, 42, 43
Behn, Noel, 63
Bennett, Arnold, 81
Bergman, Andrew, 100
Berkeley, Anthony, 10
The Big Kiss Off of 1944, 100
The Big Sleep, 99
Billy Yank, 24, 25
Bishop in Check, 56
The Bitter Harvest, 79
Blake, Nicholas, 36
The Blank Page, 60
Bleeck, Oliver, 66

C

D

[126]

O

Oakes, Blackford, 69, 70, 71
Olivier, Sir Laurence, 85
Olura, 107
Omotoso, Kole, 92
"Open Boat," 52
The Outside Man, 61
Over the High Side, 62n
Owen, D. D. R., 96
The Ox-Bow Incident, 27–28, 94
The Oxford Gambit, 65

P

Padillo, Mike, 69
Paradise Lost, 59
The Paris Review, 81
Parker, Robert B., 36, 101, 117
The Pass Beyond Kashmir, 64
Pater, Maurice, 77
Paton, Alan, 29
Patterson, Richard North, 37, 61
Pawn in Jeopardy, 56
Percy, Walker, 59
Plath, Sylvia, 20, 23, 33
Poe, Edgar Allan, 44, 71, 92, 108
The Poison People, 78
Polanski, Roman, 91
Pope, Alexander, 49
Portrait of a Lady, 14
The Postman Always Rings Twice, 81
Powell, Anthony, 77
The Power House, 78
Proctor, Maurice, 98
The Professor's House, 36
Promised Land, 101
Proust, Marcel, 13

Puberty, 103
Puritan Pleasures of the Detective Story, 81n
Pygmalion, 59
Pynchon, Thomas, 9

Q

Queen, Ellery, 40, 90
Queen in Danger, 56
The Question of Max, 35
Quiller, 55, 73–76
The Quiller Memorandum, 73

R

Radley, Sheila, 37, 97
Rampo, Edogawa, 92
Rasselas, 54
Red Anger, 107
Reflex, 17
Rhodenbarr, Bernie, 101
Riceyman Steps, 81
"Richard Cory," 20
The River Grows Wider, 96–97
Robbe-Grillet, Alain, 11
Robinson, Edward Arlington, 19–20
Rogers, Roy, 27
Rogue Male, 64, 107
Rook's Gambit, 56
Rosemary's Baby, 13, 109
Rosenberg, Samuel, 93
Rose of Tibet, 61
A Rough Shoot, 64
Routley, Erik, 81n, 116
Rowlands, O. Llew., 92
Rubens, Peter Paul, 30, 32, 35
Ruby, Jack, 8
Running Blind, 65
Russell, Col. Charles, 76, 78

S

Saint-Saëns, Camille, 110
Salieri, Antonio, 118
Samon, Albert, 100
Sanctuary, 99
Saving the Queen, 69–70
Sayers, Dorothy, 5, 10, 12–13, 34, 35, 37, 40, 97, 98, 106
"Sayers, Lord Peter and God," 34*n*
The Scorpion's Tail, 78
The Scream, 102
Scudder, Matt, 100–101
"The Second Murder," 114
The Secret Servant, 64–65
Seeger, Pete, 110
The Seersucker Whipsaw, 67
The Seven Per Cent Solution, 93
Shaffer, Anthony, 84–85, 117
Shakespeare, William, 35, 38
Shane, 87
Sheppard, Dr. James, 11, 12
Shibumi, 36
The Shining, 39
Sick Heart River, 62
Silas Marner, 28
Simenon, Georges, 41, 42–43
Simon, Roger L., 100
"The Simple Art of Murder," 88–89
The Sinkiang Executive, 74
The Sins of the Fathers, 101
Sister Carrie, 81
Sjöwall, Maj, 41, 42
Sleuth, 84
Smiley, George, 53
Snow, C. P., 81, 119
The Snow Tiger, 65
The Soft Talkers, 60
Soviet Union, 41

Spade, Sam, 40, 101
Spillane, Mickey, 67, 69*n*, 92
Spenser, 36, 101
Spy fiction, 45–79
SS-GB, 73
Stagecoach, 27
Stained Glass, 70
Stein, Gertrude, 119
Stevens, Wallace, 17–18
Stevenson, Robert Louis, 38
Stewart, J. I. M., 36
Stout, Rex, 39, 66, 81
The Strange Case of Peter the Lett, 61
The Striker Portfolio, 73
Suspicious Characters, 34
Symons, Julian, 116

T

Takagi, Akimitsu, 92
The Tango Briefing, 76
Taste of Honey, 39
Taylor, Wendell, 34
The Telemann Touch, 77
Ten Little Indians, 62*n*
Ten Little Niggers, 62*n*
Tess of the d'Urbervilles, 32, 58, 109
Thackeray, William, 81
Thérèse Raquin, 80–81
"Thirteen Ways of Looking at a Blackbird," 18
The Thirty-Nine Steps, 49, 50, 58
Thomas, Ross, 66–67, 69, 117
Thomson, June, 37
Thoreau, Henry David, 41
The Times Literary Supplement, 32
Time to Murder and Create, 101

A historian by trade, R O B I N W . W I N K S is Master
of Berkeley College, Yale University. His special fields
are British, American, and comparative history, especially
race relations, imperial studies, and historiography. Born
at West Lafayette, Indiana in 1930, he has been on the
Yale faculty since 1957. He served as Cultural Attache
at the American Embassy in London, 1969–1971. His
reviews of detective fiction are a regular feature of *The
New Republic.*

MODUS OPERANDI

has been set by Maryland Linotype Composition Company, Baltimore, Maryland, in Bodoni Book, a face named after Giambattista Bodoni (1740–1813), the son of a Piedmontese printer. After gaining renown and experience as superintendent of the Press of Propaganda in Rome, Bodoni became head of the ducal printing house of Parma in 1768. A great innovator in type design, his faces are known for their openness and delicacy.

MODUS OPERANDI has been designed by Kathleen Westray and printed on Warren's #66 Antique, an entirely acid-free paper. Haddon Craftsmen, Scranton, Pennsylvania was the printer and binder.